FASHION FABRICS: 1960s

Leslie Piña & Constance Korosec

Schiffer Publishing Ltd

4880 Lower Valley Rd. Atglen, PA 19310 USA

Copyright © 1998 by Leslie Piña & Constance Korosec
Library of Congress Catalog Card Number: 98-84472

Designed by Leslie Piña
Layout by Bonnie M. Hensley

ISBN: 0-7643-0584-0
Printed in China

Published by Schiffer Publishing Ltd.
4880 Lower Valley Road
Atglen, PA 19310
Phone: (610) 593-1777; Fax: (610) 593-2002
E-mail: Schifferbk@aol.com

In Europe, Schiffer books are distributed by Bushwood Books
6 Marksbury Avenue Kew Gardens
Surrey TW9 4JF England
Phone: 44 (0)181 392-8585; Fax: 44 (0)181 392-9876
E-mail: Bushwd@aol.com

Please write for a free catalog.
This book may be purchased from the publisher.
Please include $3.95 for shipping. Please try your bookstore first.
We are interested in hearing from authors with book ideas on related subjects.

TABLE OF CONTENTS

Acknowledgments

We would like to express our thanks to the anonymous sources and to the following who so generously provided fabrics for us to photograph for this book: American Fabrics, Barbara Cook, Lois Epstein, Fabric Centers of America, Shirley Friedland, Dorothy Johnson, Roger Josephson, May Brown Korosec, Herman Miller Inc., Deborah Rogers, Irene Sladewski, and the Ursuline College Resource Library.

Thanks again to Ramón for his assistance with the photography; to the Ursuline College library staff; to Peter Schiffer, Douglas Congdon-Martin, and the gang at Schiffer publishing.

Introduction

Fabrics can represent an era or a decade as well as any item of material culture can. The colors, patterns, textures, and fibers reveal as much about the culture as do the furnishings and clothing that relied on the fabrics. The decade of the 1960s was one of extremes. Social and cultural changes were dramatic, moving from the conservative early '60s to the radical later years of the Vietnam War. Fashion is among the most visual and widespread indicators of social conditions and change, and textiles and their design naturally influence fashion.

Some fabrics are more quickly associated with the 1960s than others. Plaids, though very popular, are traditional patterns, and these were reintroduced rather than introduced. At the other extreme, bold prints and geometrics, notably Op Art and "psychedelic" patterns and colors, could hardly be from any other time. Exaggerated textures and novelty knits, though introduced earlier, became more varied and more abundant in the '60s. Synthetics, also introduced earlier, took off during the decade, and phrases like "polyester knit" and "stretch knit" elicit visions of unmistakably '60s staples. Textured acetate, triacetate, nylon, polyester and acrylic became a new factor in fashion offering yarns literally engineered to suit the concepts of the fashion designer.

The following highlights of 1960's fabric innovations and events, mostly from the pages of *American Fabrics* magazine, will help to introduce the hundreds of examples of fashion fabrics presented here. There are many good publications about textiles that include technical and historical information, and some of these are listed in the Bibliography. But since the only way to experience the fabric of a decade is to see it, this book is entirely dedicated to the sensory — the visual delight. The authors hope that the reader will enjoy seeing these miniature historic design documents and works of graphic art and textile virtuosity as much as we enjoyed presenting them.

1960

- Pucci popularizes "silk" stretch pants. The fabric had a stretch nylon warp with a silk sub-filling. It became top fashion news throughout the world and launched the boom in women's stretch pants.

- American Viscose Corporation stated that in 1910 there was only one type of rayon and two end-products. In 1960 there were 109 types of rayon with hundreds of uses.

- Firestone Tire & Rubber Company announced the formation of its Molded Fiber Products Division. Fibrocast was the name chosen for the products.

- The Australian wool-selling season is to be extended to the full twelve months of the year due to an increase in demand. Australia was enjoying record breaking production of wool.

- Industrial Rayon Corporation announced its third fiber, polypropylene, under the name of "Prolene." It came in staple fiber, tow, and continuous filament. Industrial Rayon was one of the largest producers of nylon and rayon. The home of the new fiber was Covington, Va., while the pilot plant was located in Cleveland, Ohio.

- Celanese Corporation of America bought Darvan nytril fiber from B.F. Goodrich Company, Cleveland, Ohio. The purchase included patents, trademarks, technical service, and world rights to produce and market the fiber. Darvan resulted from research done during World War II.

- American Viscose Corporation announced a new type of cellulosic fiber, Avlin. The fiber owed its properties to a new spinning technique that tended to flatten the yarn, giving it a triangular rather than a conventional round cross-section. The name, Avlin, was applied to the fiber as well as to the fabrics made from it, which have a linen-like look.

- 1960 was the bicentennial of the United States woolen textile industry. In 1760 the Colonies began the manufacture of woolen cloth in textile mills in New England. American Heritage Wools was the keynote for the observance which was sponsored by Woolens and Worsteds of America.

- American Viscose Corporation's aid to education for the year benefitted 83 colleges and universities. The recipients for the scholarships were selected by the respective schools.

- Grants totaling more than $1.3 million were awarded to 143 universities and colleges in the United States in the DuPont annual program of aid to education. The program was for fundamental research by universities to strengthen the teaching of science and related subjects, and for education or research in science and engineering.

- The new fiber, Alon, was unveiled in the United States. Alon is a trademark name of Toyo Rayon Company, Ltd., Osaka, Japan. It is a cellulose fiber and was marketed by the Star Woolen Company, Cohoes, New York.

- The first cotton mill west of the Mississippi River was located in Casa Grande, Arizona, formed by Eastern and Southern mill interests. The name of the new plant was Kimberly Mills.

- The Wall Street Journal reported that, according to Davidson's Textile Blue Book, there were 9,242 individual textile plants in the United States in 1953, compared to 8,470 in 1960.

- Fiber Industries, Inc., announced the new name, Fortrel, to replace Teron polyester fiber. The plant of the concern was in Shelby, N.C., and the company was a joint venture of Celanese Corporation of America and Imperial Chemical Industries, Ltd., Great Britain.

- The United States Olympic Team was outfitted in wash-and-wear dress uniforms when it traveled to Rome for the Olympics. The fabric content was 70% Acrilan blended with acetate and rayon.

- The Textile Fiber Products Identification Act, approved by Congress, September 2nd, 1959, went into effect on the third of March, 1960.

- DuPont announced its Type 288 nylon, which had been engineered for commercial texturizing equipment. The new yarn had improved bulk, dyeing uniformity and strength retention under mill and consumer use.

- Man-made fibers continued their meteoric rise in total fiber consumption. Total consumption in 1959 was 1.9 billion pounds.

- Canadian Celanese, Ltd., announced its new polyolefin fiber, Propylon. This fiber was said to be lighter than other man-made fibers, having good resistance to abrasion and unaffected by water and most of the common chemicals.

- Deering Milliken & Company, Inc., announced a new type of wash-and-wear men's shirt introduced by Cluett, Peabody & Co. The shirting was made of Belfast "self-ironing" cotton.

- The rise of textured filament yarn in the carpet industry was meteoric. In 1958 only 500,000 pounds were used in the United States; in 1959 the total amounted to three million pounds with a prediction of 30 million pounds for 1961.

- Owens-Corning Fiberglas Corporation announced a glass fiber with approximately 50% greater rigidity, without lessening strength.

- New nonionic pigment padding colors were offered for dyeing cottons and synthetics in pastel and medium shades. Outstanding features included excellent compatibility and versatility; they could be run alone, with various auxiliaries, or in most resin finishing baths.

- Introduction the Hisperse dispersion, a significant advance in the technology of disperse dyes.

1961

- Knit industry yarn consumption was 865 million pounds.

- The French developed textured acetate which opened up the whole dress market to the use of these elegant, silk-like textured yarns.

- Ticking fabrics used in sportswear; tweeds were popular.

1962

- "Bubble Piqué" was an entirely new look of blistered effect on cloth.

- Textured sweaters were shown with shiny black leather; denim used as a fashion statement.

- New Aquaprint Colors and Clears were formulated to further reduce crocking in printing with pigmented emulsions.

- Application of the Hisperse techniques to the Polydye line, resulting in improved colors for the dyeing of polyester fibers.

- World production of man-made textile fibers totaled 8,921 million pounds; world production of natural textile fibers totaled 26,383 million pounds.

1963

- World production of man-made textile fibers totaled 9,918 million pounds; world production of natural textile fibers totaled 27, 560 millions pounds.

- White wool pantsuits shown with white leather boots.

- India Madras became so popular that most importers were booked up to the end of the Spring 1965 season and were hard-pressed to keep the fabric in stock. During the fiscal year which ended in March 1963, India exported 13,500,000 yards of India Madras fabric to the United States.

1964

- Knit industry yarn consumption 1090 million pounds.

- World production of man-made textile fibers total 11,278 million pounds; world production of natural textile fibers total 28,256 million pounds.

- First introduction of HiFast colors, marking a breakthrough in roller printing of synthetics and blends.

1965

- World production of man-made textile fibers total 12,203 million pounds; world production of natural textile fibers total 28,456 million pounds.

- Major textile mills:
  Burlington
  J.P. Stevens
  United Merchants
  Deering-Milliken
  West Point-Pepperell
  Lowenstein
  Cannon Mills
  Cone Mills
  Springs Cottons
  Dan River Mills
  Beaunit
  Collins & Aikman
  Reeves Brothers
  Riegel Textile Co.
  Graniteville Co.

- Major fiber producers:
  DuPont
  Union Carbide
  Monsanto (Chemstrand)
  Kodak (Tenn. Eastman)
  U.S. Rubber
  Dow Chemical
  Allied Chemical

FMC Corporation (American Viscose)
American Cyanamid
Celanese Corp.
Hercules
Owens Corning
American Enka
Beaunit

1966

- Different fabric textures shown together; the metal-link plastic disc dress and the plastic dress shown.

- World production of man-made textile fibers total 13,308 million pounds; world production of natural textile fibers total 26,065 million pounds.

- Full scale programming of the HiFast system after two years of plant operation.

- Polydye SF colors were introduced. These disperse dyes were created especially to meet the industry demands for products withstanding permanent press finishing on polyester cellulose blends.

- New cloth development "Durango," permanent press of fine combed 2-ply yarns.

- One of the most significant trends in the youth movement is a greater emphasis on dresses:
  Tent Dress
  High-rise shift
  Square trapeze
  Geometric dress
  Tunic dress
  T-shirt dress
  Dress that hangs from the shoulder
  Wrap-over dress
  Long-sleeved trapeze
  Bias chemise in chiffon
  Convict-striped sweater dress
  Bi-color and tri-color dress
  Smock dress

- The major soil release systems with date and name of product:
  June 1966 VISA — Deering Milliken (casual slacks and tablecloths)
  September 1966 FYBRITE — Celanese (lingerie, shirtings, printed dresses, knitted polyester uniforms)
  January 1967 COME CLEAN — Burlington (Klopman) (tablecloths, curtains, shirts, pants)
  January 1967 X-IT — McCampbell-Graniteville (work shirts, work pants, casual slacks)
  May 1967 DUAL-ACTION SCOTCHGARD — 3M (casual slacks, sport shirts, dresses, sportswear and work clothing)

1967

- African prints popular for dresses; psychedelic and ethnic fashions appear in designer collections.

- The no-iron sheet takes on a significant portion of the sheet industry.

- Knitted stretch fabric coverings are used for free-form furniture.

- Hilton-Davis announces Lifebond colors, a dramatic breakthrough in pigment printing systems.

1968

- World production of rayon and acetate fiber 7.7 billion pounds; United States production 1.6 billion.

- World production of nylon fiber 3.6 billion pounds; United States production 1.3 billion.

- World production of acrylic fiber 1.6 billion pounds; United States production .52 billion.

- World fiber production of polyester 2.4 billions of pounds; United States production 1.1 billion.

- World production of man-made textile fibers total 16,165 million pounds; world production of natural textile fibers total 25,770 million pounds.

- Crimped HWM rayon with improved covering power developed by FMC-American Viscose.

- A permanent flame retardant (PFR) rayon developed by FMC-American Viscose research.

1969

- There are 4,388 tricot machines in 98 tricot mills and 3,432 raschel machines in 124 raschel mills in the United States.

- Flocking in advanced and sophiscated forms begins to emerge as an important technology in textile production.

- Allied Chemical prepares to enter the polyester market with a new plant capable of producing 80 million pounds of polyester fiber annually.

- Fabrics from sugar cane are produced experimentally in Rumania. Chemical cellulose is extracted from the cane and processed by methods similar to those used to make rayon.

CHAPTER 1:

SOLIDS & TEXTURES

100% silk linen.
Early 1960s.

100% silk linen.
Early 1960s.

100% silk
crinkled crepe.
Stehli Silks.
1960.

50/50 Fortrel,
cotton.
Virginia Mills.
1963.

100% wool.
Mid 1960s.

100% silk linen.
Early 1960s.

50% Vycron
polyester, 50%
Avron rayon.
Beaunit, Inc.
1960.

Rayon, cotton
Veltessa, in high
fashion hearth
red.
Crompton-
Richmond.
1960.

75% Tusson
rayon, 25% silk.
Westerhoff.
1961.

71% cotton, 29%
nylon, stretch
denim.
Cone.
1964.

Fortrel polyester, cotton, nylon, rayon, stretch denim. Erwin. 1969.

Fortrel polyester, cotton, nylon, rayon, stretch denim. Erwin. 1969.

100% cotton yarn-dyed red/ white oxford; fabric was specially woven for Sero of New Haven. J.P. Stevens. 1960.

50% Kodel polyester, 50% cotton corduroy. Cone Mills, Inc. 1965.

Cotton nylon blend, stretch tweed denim. Swift Mfg. Co. 1965.

100% wool. Ria Herlinger Fabrics, Inc. 1961.

100% raw silk. Late 1960s.

Flax cotton blend. Crompton-Richmond. 1962.

70% Quintess polyester double knit; a Phillips 66 fiber, 30% imported Irish linen. 1968.

72% acetate, 28% Mylar. Security. 1965.

Worsted wool woven.
Einiger.
1961.

Silk worsted, basket weave.
By Phillip Vogelman of Onondaga.
Onondaga.
1960.

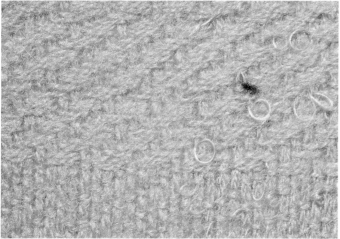

100% wool.
Ria Herlinger.
1960.

100% wool.
Ria Herlinger.
1961.

100% wool.
Mid 1960s.

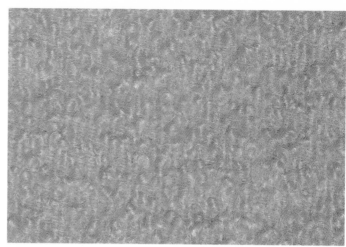

100% wool, basket weave.
Hanora Fabrics.
1962.

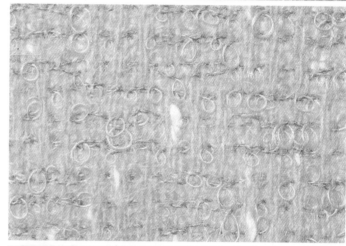

Fiberglas Beta glass yarn.
By Titus Blatter.
Owens-Corning Fiberglas Corp.
1963.

100% cotton, knitted look in corduroy.
Crompton-Richmond.
1961.

100% wool.
Mid 1960s.

Linen, cotton, viscose.
Crestwood Corp.
1963.

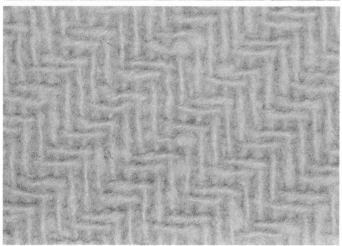

100% Orlon acrylic.
Shulman Fabrics.
1964.

100% wool, step-ladder weave.
Einiger Mills.
1962.

100% Creslan acrylic.
Greeff.
1964.

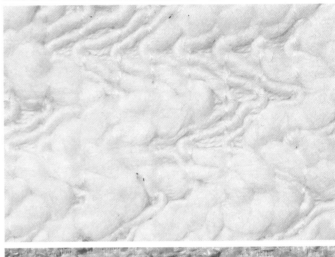

100% cotton.
Earl-loom.
1964.

Fiberglas Beta glass yarn by Seneca Textile.
Owens-Corning Fiberglas Corp.
1963.

60% cotton, 40% Antron.
Inwood Knitting Mills.
1964.

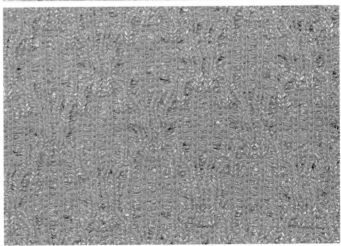

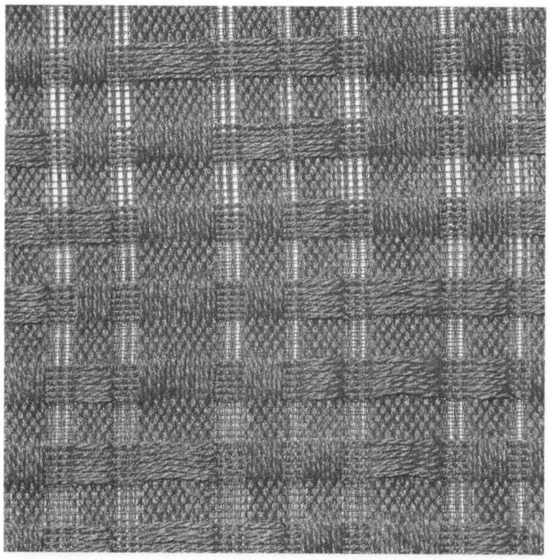

85% cotton, 15% silk.
House of Individual Fabrics.
1964.

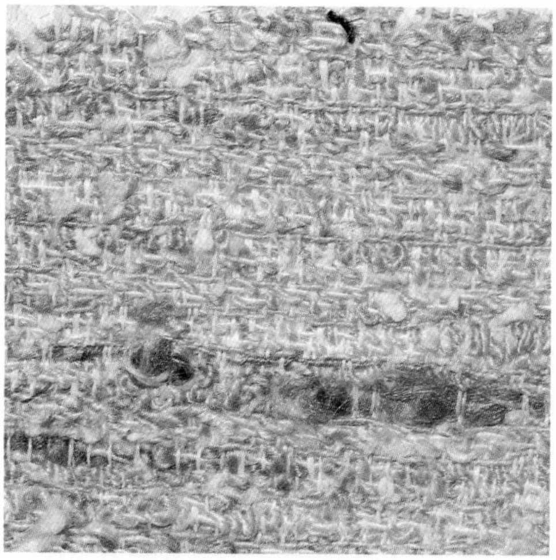

70% Avisco rayon, 24% acetate, 6% silk.
Cohama.
1964.

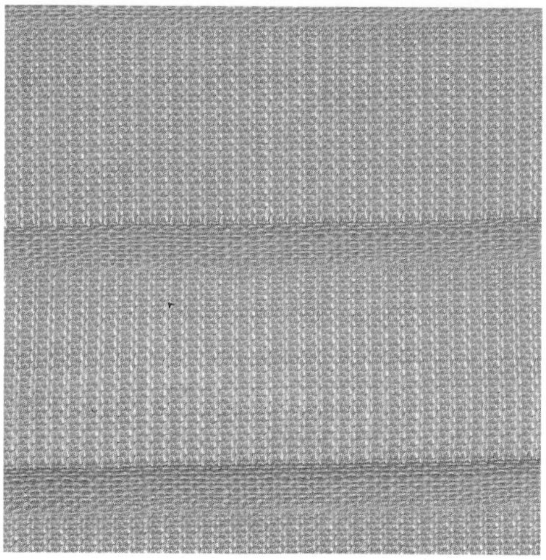

100% cotton.
Galey & Lord.
1964.

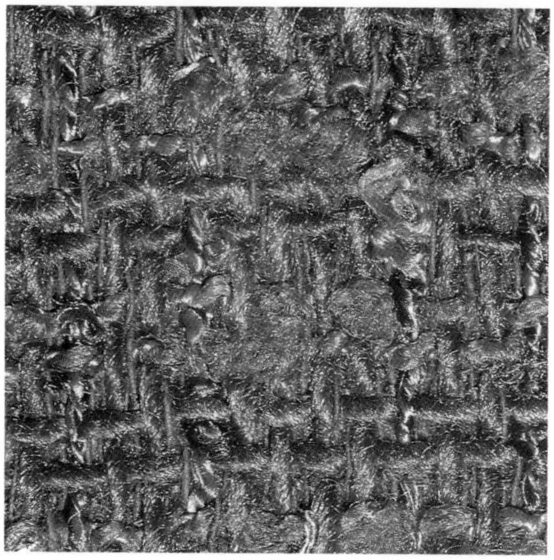

Rayon, acetate, cotton.
Cohama.
1965.

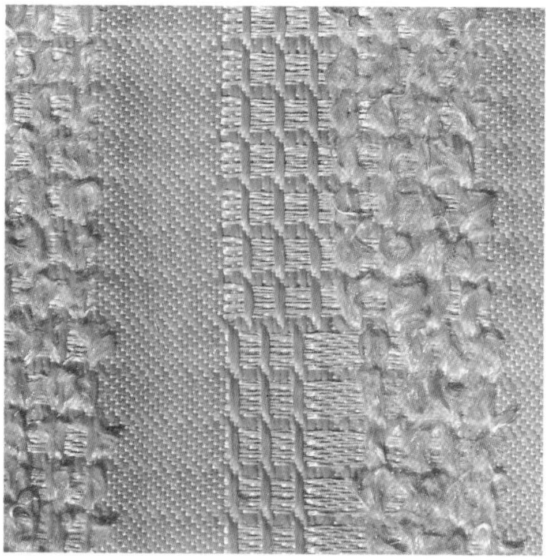

Rayon, acetate, nylon blend, bouclé weave.
American Silk Mills.
1961.

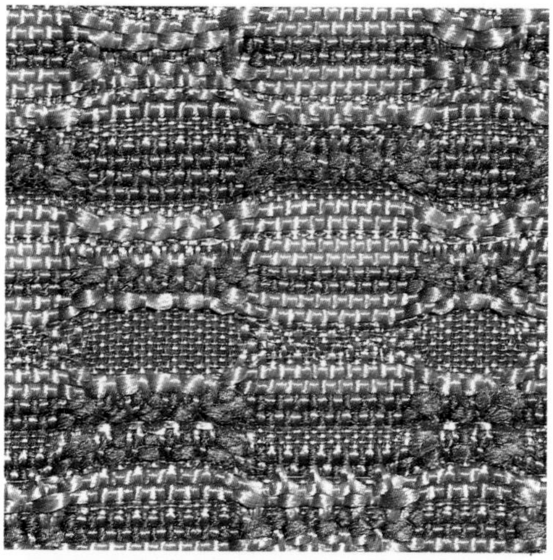

Automotive fabric, woven.
Collins & Aikman.
1961.

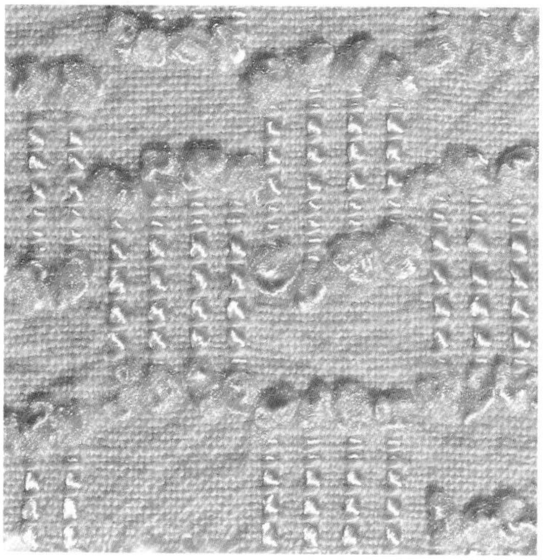

100% cotton frieze texture.
Morgan-Jones Mills.
1960.

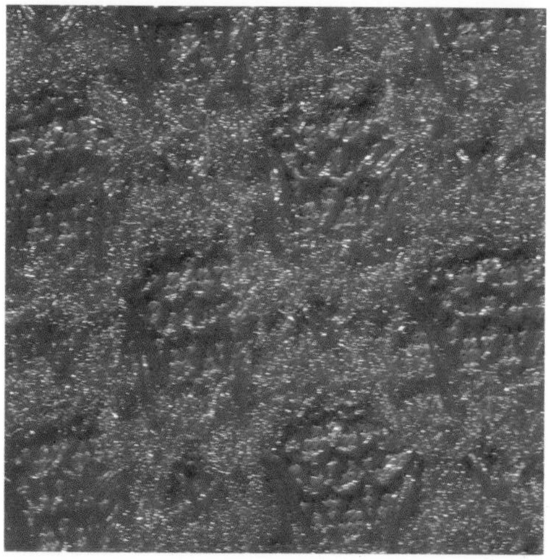

100% Antron nylon.
Lancer.
1965.

520 Denier rib knit,
bouclé yarns.
Bucaroni .
1965.

Cotton flamme,
wool worsted.
New Editions,
Inc.
1967.

Polyester rayon,
Avril rayon yarns.
Burlington.
1966.

Rayon, silk
blend.
Reliable Textiles.
1964.

Viscose, cotton,
rayon.
Quaker Corpora-
tion.
1966.

100% cotton,
Jacquard
weave.
Everfast.
1961.

Cotton, linen and
rayon blend.
Security Mills.
1965.

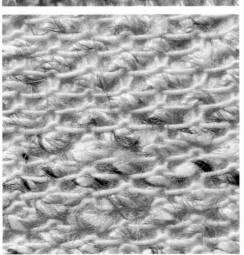

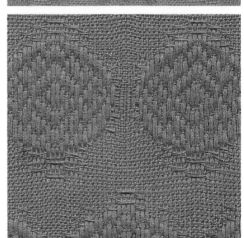

100% cotton,
Dobby weave.
Wamsutta.
1961.

Wool for color,
Taslan nylon for
bulk.
Bernati.
1961.

Cotton and nylon.
Security Mills.
1966.

Nylon, Antron,
stretch matelassé.
Travis Fabric.
Mid 1960s.

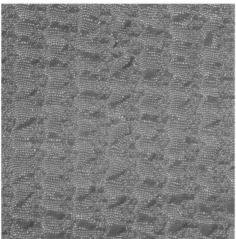

Vinyl.
Cooney-Weiss
Fabric Corp.
1966.

Acetate, Avesco
rayon.
Onondaga Silk Co.
1965.

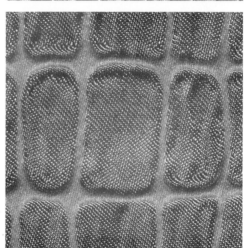

100% acetate,
alligator, lizard
inspired by Stehli.
Earl-Glo.
1963.

Chemstitch velvet.
J.B. Martin.
1967.

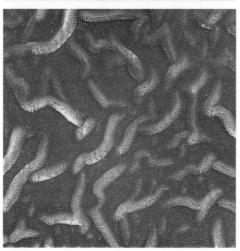

100% nylon wet
look.
N. Erlanger,
Blumgart & Co.
1967.

16

100% silk Dupioni; imported from Italy. Republic Commercial. 1960.

100% wool. Mid 1960s.

100% iridescent silk Shantung. Jacobson. 1960.

Denim, herring-bone weave. Erwin Mills. 1969.

100% wool. Mid 1960s.

100% wool. Mid 1960s.

100% wool. Mid 1960s.

100% Wool. Mid 1960s.

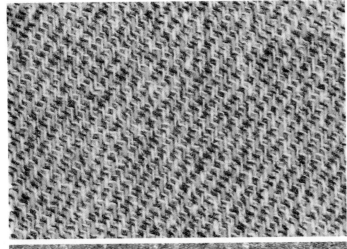

100% wool.
The Erchless.
Guilford.
1962.

100% Creslan acrylic .
Troy Mills.
1965.

81% rayon, 14% acetate, 5% silk.
Rosewood.
1966.

Fortrel polyester, rayon, silk.
Julius N. Werk.
1963.

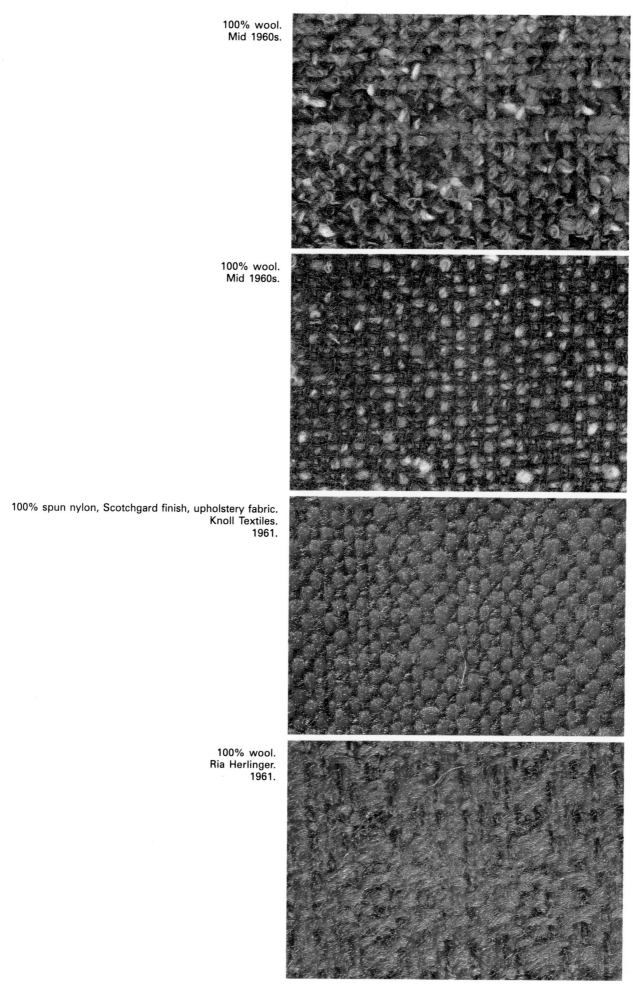

100% wool.
Mid 1960s.

100% wool.
Mid 1960s.

100% spun nylon, Scotchgard finish, upholstery fabric.
Knoll Textiles.
1961.

100% wool.
Ria Herlinger.
1961.

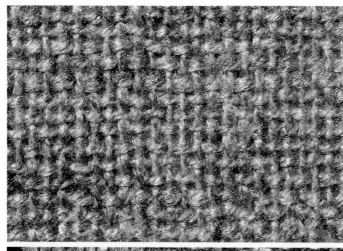

60% Viscose, 20% nylon, 20% acrylic bonded to tricot of 100% acetate.
Guilford Woolen Fabrics.
1965.

Wool, mohair, cotton tweed.
Scotney Mills.
1963.

Caprolan nylon.
C.L. Meyers Co., Inc.
1966.

100% wool.
Berroco.
1963.

100% wool loose weave.
Anglo.
1960.

100% wool.
Earl-Craft.
1962.

Bulked cotton, acetate yarn, flat crochet weave.
Concord Textile Co.
1964.

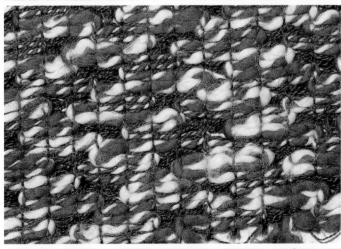

Mohair.
Lawrence D. Gabbe, Inc.
1964.

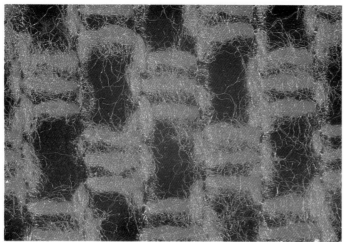

Acetate velvet ribbon, brushed Orlon yarn.
Novelty Textile Mills.
1966.

Wool, mohair.
Yuma Woolen Mills.
1964.

Synthetic blend.
Guilford Fabrics, Inc.
1967.

Nylon, viscose tweed.
Guilford Fabrics, Inc.
1965.

Acetate bonded.
Einiger.
1965.

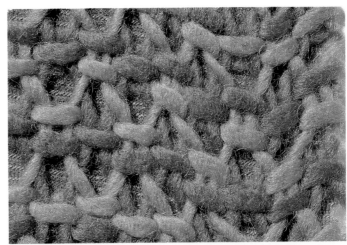

100% wool.
Yuma Woolen Mills.
1966.

70% Dacron, 30% wool.
Novelty Textile Mills.
1969.

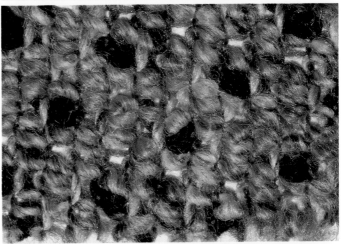

Dacron bonded.
Guilford.
1965.

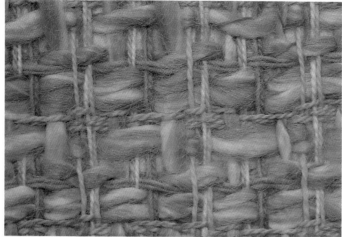

83% acrylic, 17% cotton.
Herlinger-Bristol.
1968.

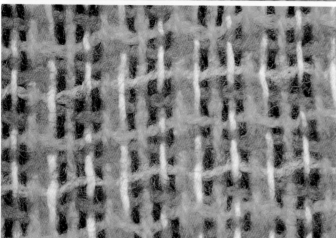

89% wool worsted, 11% Acrilan.
Herlinger-Bristol.
1967.

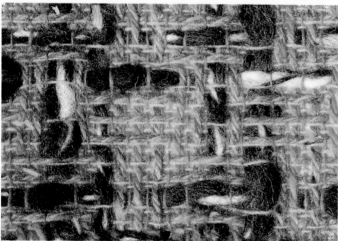

Blend.
American Iwer Corp.
1967.

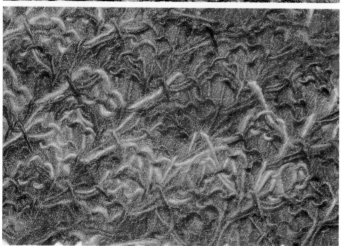

Bonded fabric.
Knitbrook.
1968.

Blended.
Lawford Fabrics.
1960.

100% wool.
St. Patrick Woolen Mills of Ireland.
1964.

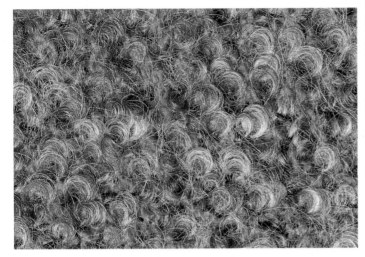

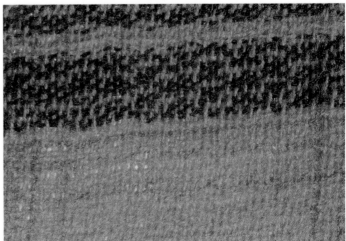

100% wool, variation crepe weave.
Ria Herlinger.
1963.

Wool.
Wedgmoor Woolens.
1965.

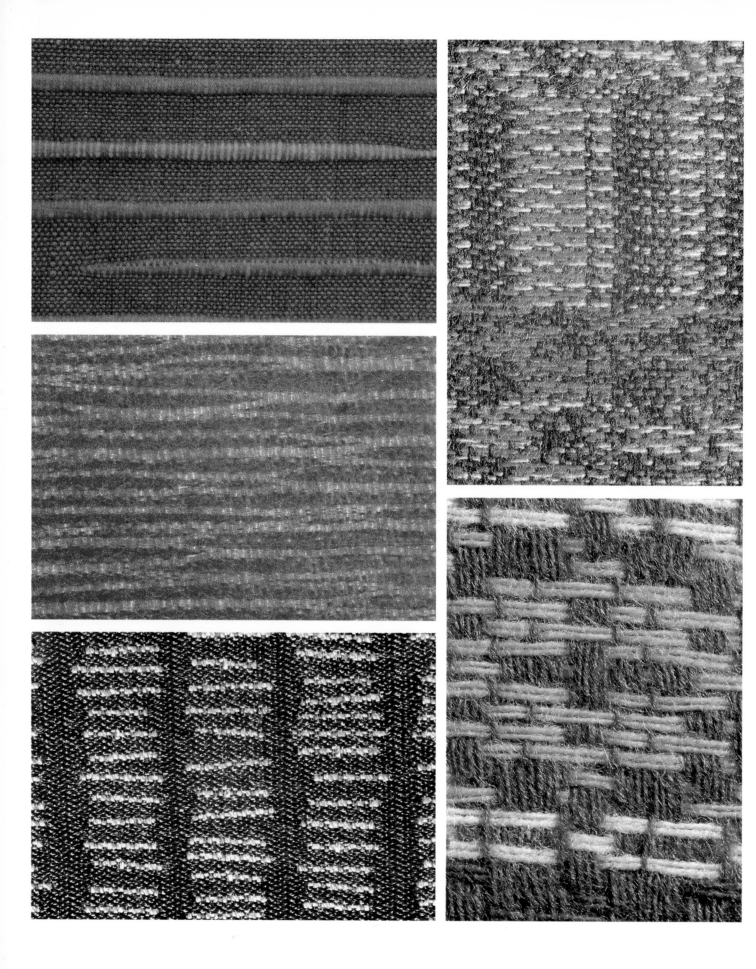

Opposite page:
Top left: 100% cotton hand loomed in India by Comtrust. Parry Murray & Co. 1969.

Center left: Creslan wool. Virginia Mills for Jacques Maisch. 1963.

Bottom left: Auto upholstery. Collins & Aikman. 1961.

Top right: 50/50 blend of Creslan acrylic, wool. Exclusive Fabrics. 1961.

Bottom right: 100% wool. Woolmark. 1961.

63% Creslan acrylic, 32% wool, 5% nylon. Milliken. 1964.

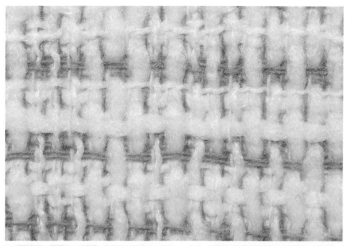

100% wool, Leno weave. Anglo Fabrics. 1961.

Wool knit. Novelty Textile Mills. 1967.

Creslan acrylic fiber, mohair. American Cyanamid. 1965.

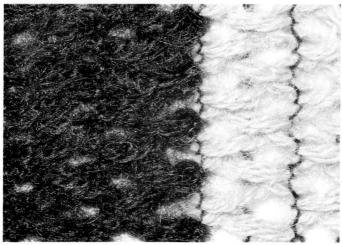

Taslan textured nylon.
Sesom Knitting Mills.
1965.

Fiberglas Beta glass yarn.
Owens-Corning Fiberglas Corp.
1963.

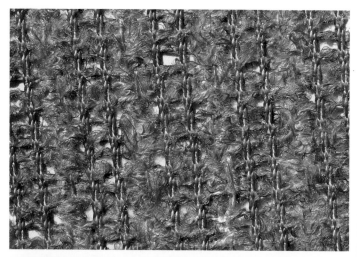

Celanese knit.
Dixie Yarns, Inc.
1965.

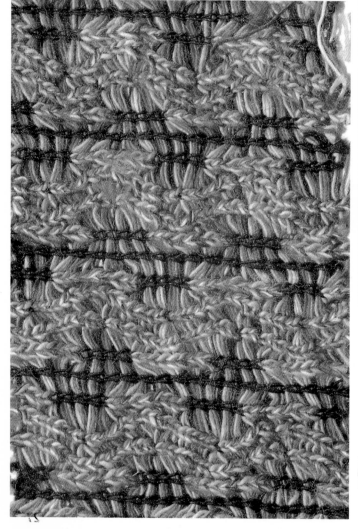

100% combed cotton.
Inwood Knitting Mills.
1964.

35% acetate, 65% rayon.
Cohama.
1967.

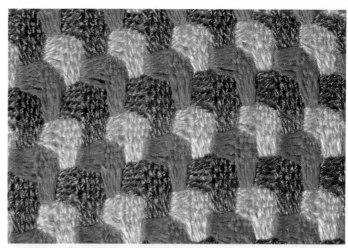

100% cotton.
Collins & Aikman.
1969.

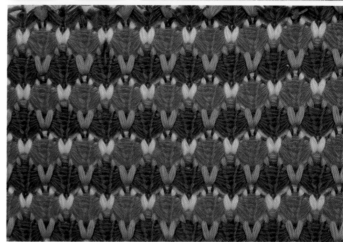

100% cotton.
Originit.
1960.

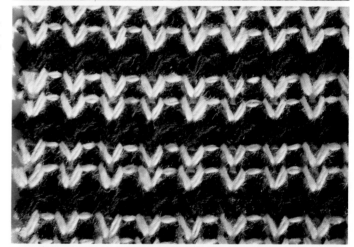

100% wool.
Stanley Woolen Co.
1960.

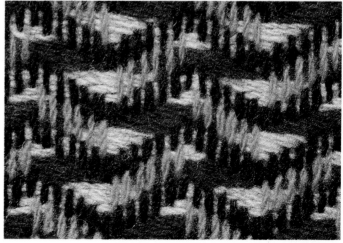

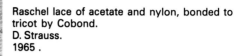

CHAPTER 2

NOVELTY

Raschel lace of acetate and nylon, bonded to
tricot by Cobond.
D. Strauss.
1965 .

Point d' Esprit, hand-clipped silk lace.
Stern & Stern.
1960.

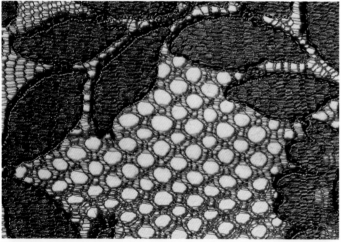

100% nylon, hand-clipped textured Alencon lace.
Wiener Laces.
1961.

Cluny-type lace.
Stern & Stern.
1966.

85% spun rayon, 10% flax, 5% nylon.
Everfast.
1967.

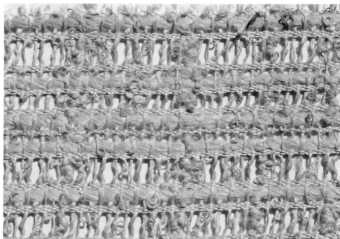

Fiberglas, woven by Hess Goldsmith.
Burlington.
1962.

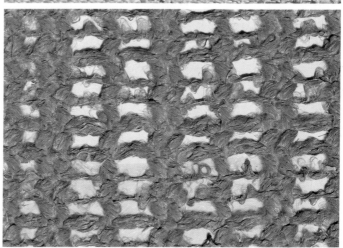

Fiberglas Beta glass yarn.
Milton H. Stern.
Owens-Corning Fiberglas Corp.
1963.

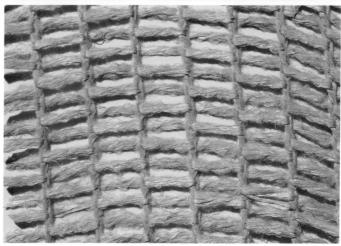

Fiberglas Beta glass yarn.
QualFab.
Owens-Corning Fiberglas Corp.
1963.

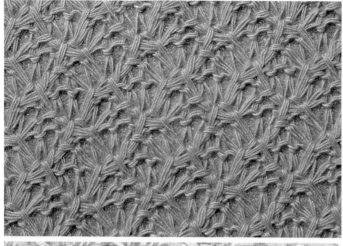

50% Kodel, 50% cotton.
Acadia Co.
1965.

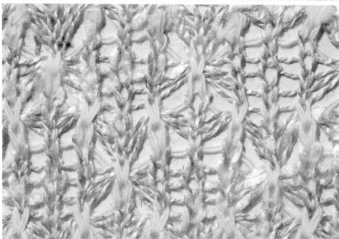

Linen/rayon/cotton blend.
Berman Fabrics.
1965.

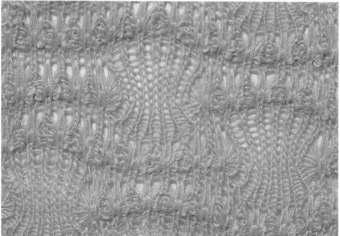

100% Creslan.
Spilke & Sons, Inc.
1963.

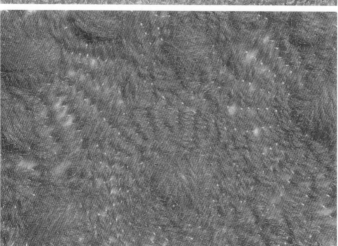

Orlon on sheer nylon.
United Embroidery.
1967.

100% Durene cotton.
Hopknits.
1965.

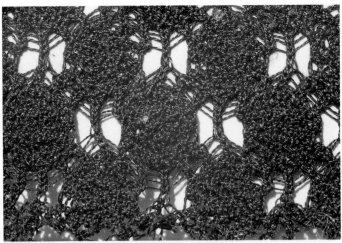

85% Orlon, 10% nylon, 5% cotton.
George Richardson Inc.
1967.

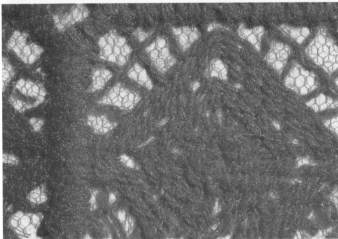

Lacy pinwheel knit, 80% Orlon acrylic,
10% DuPont nylon, 10% cotton.
DuPont.
1965.

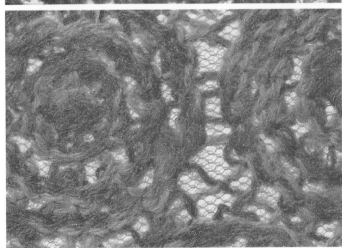

100% Orlon.
DuPont.
1965.

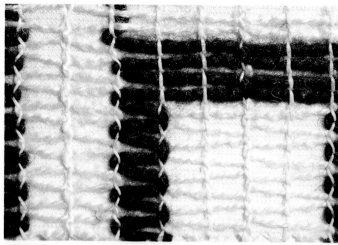

68% Viscose rayon, 32% acrylic.
Guilford Fabrics.
1967.

100% acetate tricot.
William Heller Inc.
1965.

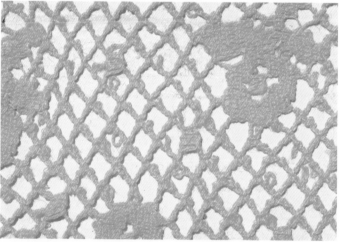

100% nylon, fishnet lace.
Stern & Stern Textiles.
1964.

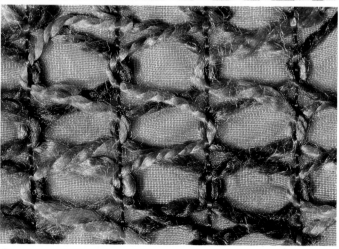

Rayon and acetate yarn.
Novelty Textile Mills.
1966.

100% Rovana saran flat filament.
Jack Lenor Larsen.
1965.

Metallic grill cloth.
Branson Co. metallic yarns.
Chicopee.
1961.

38% Caprolan nylon, 33% Coloray, 29% nylon.
Berkshire-Hathaway.
1967.

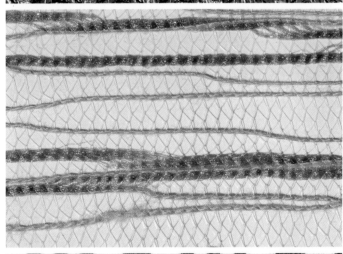

Arnel and cotton.
Richelieu.
1968.

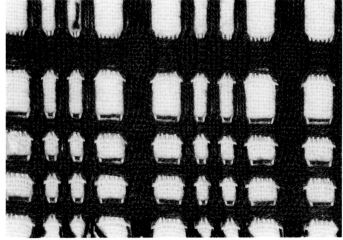

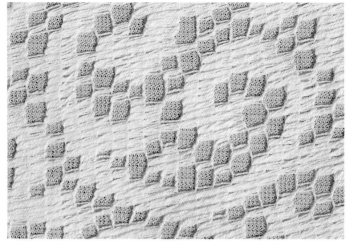

Cotton bonded.
Peacedale Processing.
1965.

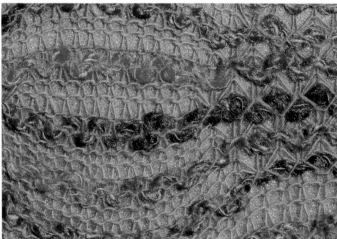

Knitted rayon, cotton yarn bonded to acetate tricot.
Security Mills.
1967.

100% Orlon.
Security Mills.
1967.

Polyester knit Op Art design.
Fabrics by Joyce.
1968.

Spun rayon brocade.
Kendale Fabrics.
1965.

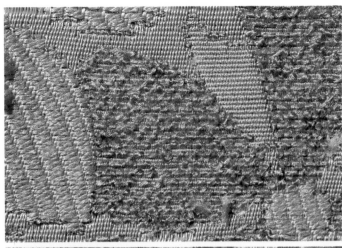

100% rayon woven.
Collins & Aikman.
1967.

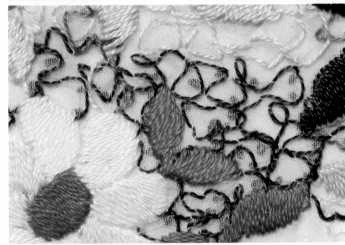

Schiffli lace.
Swisscraft.
1968.

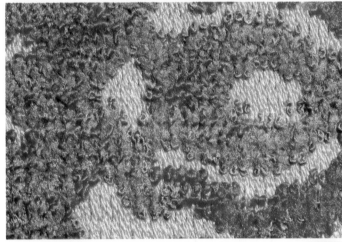

100% Orlon embroidery.
Park Schiffli.
1967.

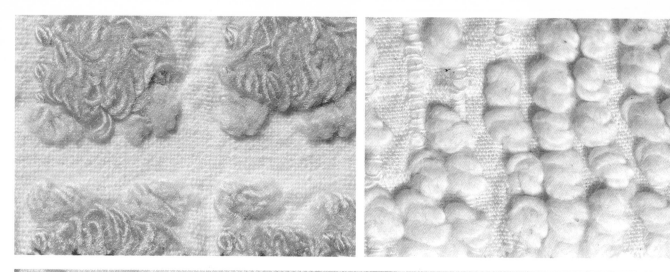

Top left: 100% cotton.
Morgan-Jones Inc.
1960.

Top right: 100% cotton.
Bates.
1965.

Bottom: Nylon taffeta.
Carolace Embroidery Co.
1965.

Dacron polyester.
Novelty Textile Mills.
1965.

Cotton eyelash.
Late 1960s.

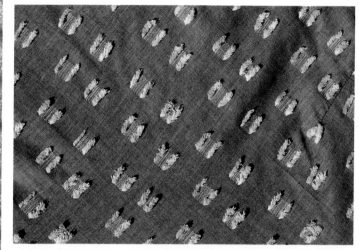

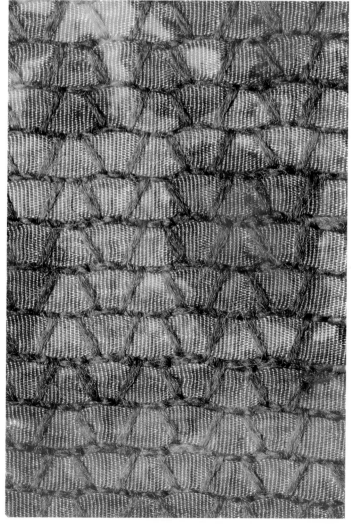

50% Fortrel, 50% cotton floating eyelash.
Dan River.
1969.

100% Acetate ribbon knit.
Stehli Silk Co.
1964.

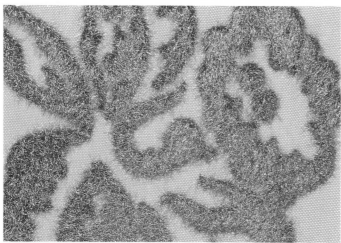

Nylon taffeta flocked pattern.
Earl-Glo.
1964.

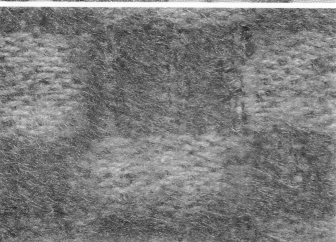

Brushed worsted wool and mohair.
Einiger.
1961.

50% Creslan, 50% Dynel modacrylic; used as a scatter rug in home furnishings.
Princeton.
1961.

100% rayon face, 100% cotton back, ponyskin.
Sidney Blumenthal.
1961.

100% Orlon face, 100% cotton back; "Tiger" man-made furs.
Princeton.
1961.

100% acrylic knit.
Collins & Aikman.
1965.

75% modacrylic, 25% mohair; Somali leopard fake fur.
Collins & Aikman.
1963.

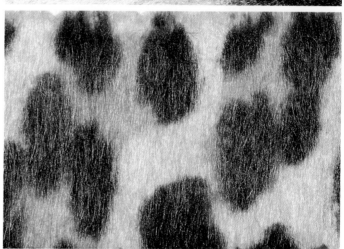

Syl-mer finish, velveteen leopard print.
Crompton.
1961.

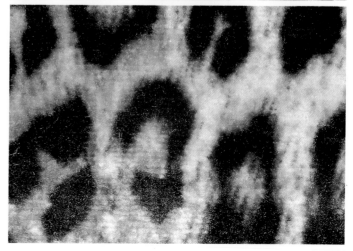

CHAPTER 3

METALLIC

Metallic knit.
Branson.
1961.

Rayon, mylar.
Hopknits.
1965.

Creslan, Avril, Lurex.
R.S.L. Fabrics Corp.
1963.

Knitted wool and metallic glitter trend.
Lebanon Mills.
1961.

Acetate tricot gunmetal fabric.
Kendale Fabrics.
1965.

Metallic brocade.
Branson Co. metallic yarns.
Tioga.
1961.

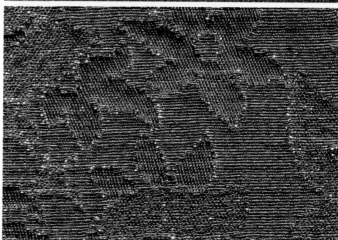

100% cotton and "mylar" yarn.
Morgan-Jones Mills.
1960.

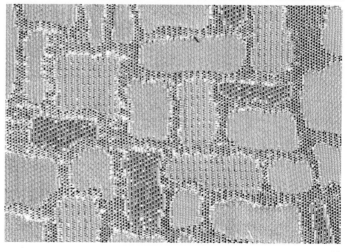

Lurex glistening jacquard.
Hawley Fabrics Co.
1969.

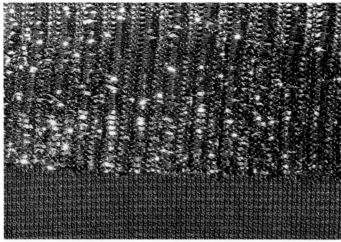

100% acetate rayon metallic yarn knit.
Xantex.
1967.

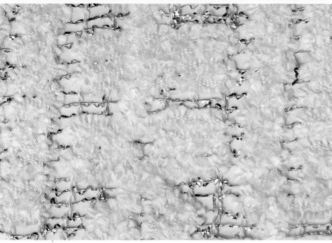

Chenille and Lurex knit.
Philipsburg Knitting Mills.
1969.

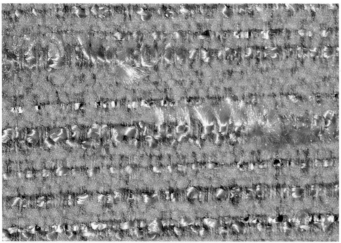

Transportation fabric for airline and bus companies.
Collins & Aikman.
1961.

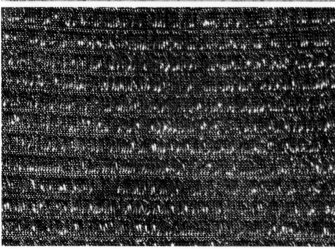

Lurex glitter knit.
Ross Zeldin Inc.
1969.

Lurex metallic yarn.
Dow Badische.
1967.

Lurex frizette yarn.
Dow Badische.
1967.

100% cotton sari cloth.
H.M. Kolbe.
1962.

80% rayon, 20% mylar.
Printed by Applikay Division.
Fabrics by Joyce.
1968.

45

53% Dacron, 47% Antron.
Stretchnit.
1967.

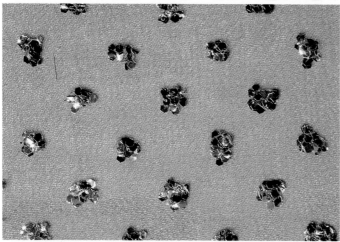

100% Viscose rayon.
Stern & Stern.
1967.

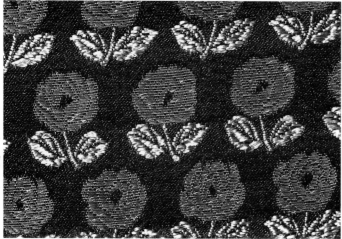

Silk brocade with rayon and metallic.
G. Hirsch Sons.
1960.

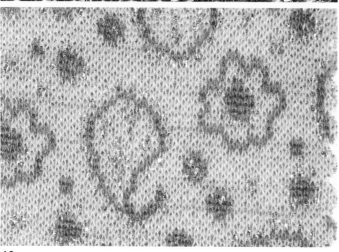

100% acrylic.
Security Mills.
Zefkrome.
1962.

100% silk
brocade.
1960.

Metallic dim luster look.
Orinoka Mills.
1965.

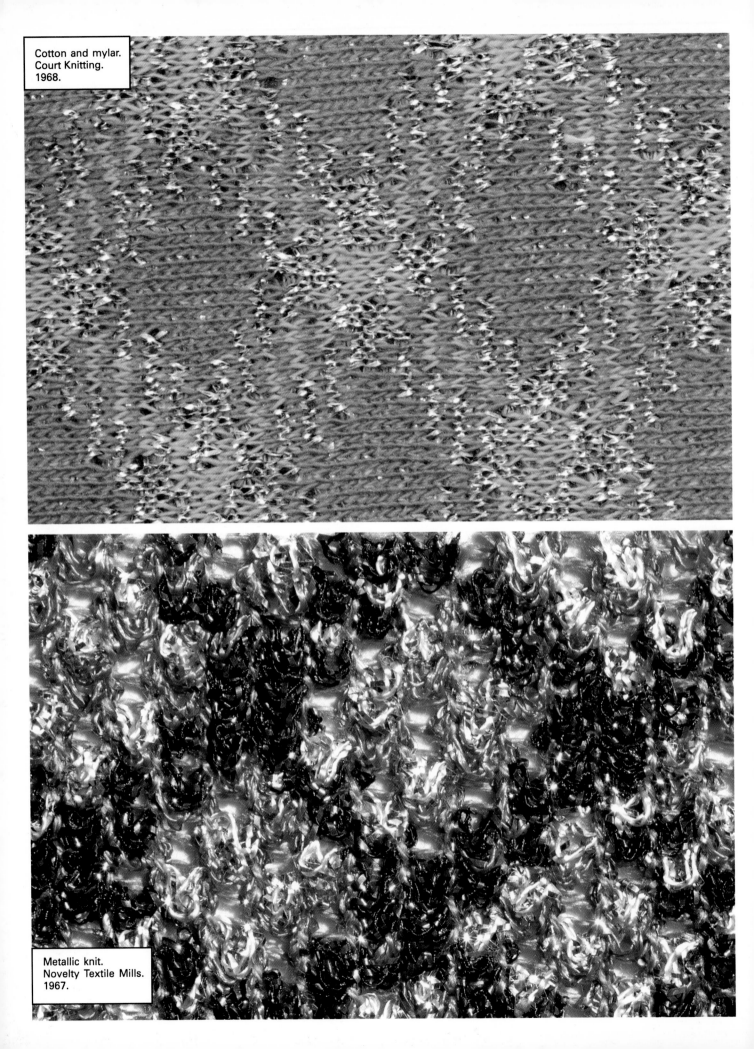

Cotton and mylar.
Court Knitting.
1968.

Metallic knit.
Novelty Textile Mills.
1967.

Gold, silver base, "Saturn"
new shoe fabric.
Nailhead Creations.
1967.

CHAPTER 4

STRIPES

Top left: 100% wool, reversible.
Ria Herlinger.
1965.

Top right: 100% wool.
Originit.
1960.

Bottom left: Wool.
Mid 1960s.

Bottom right: Preliminary color predictions.
American Fabrics Color Council.
1962.

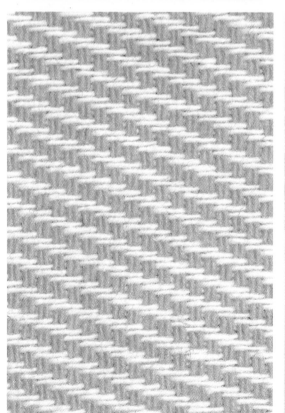

Top left: Dacron and rayon blend.
Crown Fabrics.
1962

Top right: Avron rayon.
Crown Fabrics.
1961.

Bottom left: 100% cotton.
Russell of Alabama.
1962.

Bottom right: 100% cotton.
Galey & Lord, a Division of Burlington Industries.
1961.

Denim stripe.
Erwin Mills.
1969.

Corfam for shoe leather markets.
DuPont.
1967.

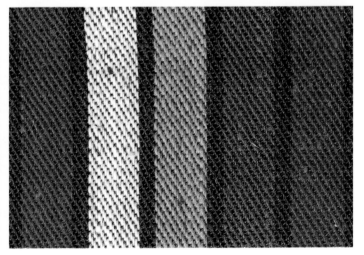

100% cotton denim stripe.
Avondale.
1960.

100% silk double warp.
Catoir Silk.
1960.

Top left: 100% cotton. Everfast. 1961.

Top right: 50% Kodel, 50% cotton. Deering Milliken Co. Mill. Crown Textile Fabrics. 1960.

50-50 blend, Orlon acrylic and rayon. United States Rubber. 1960.

50% Acrilan acrylic, 50% rayon. U.S. Royal. 1960.

100% Creslan acrylic.
Troy Mills, Inc.
1963.

Silk and mercerized cotton.
Fred J. Kern Textiles.
1960.

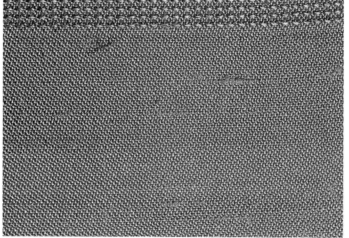

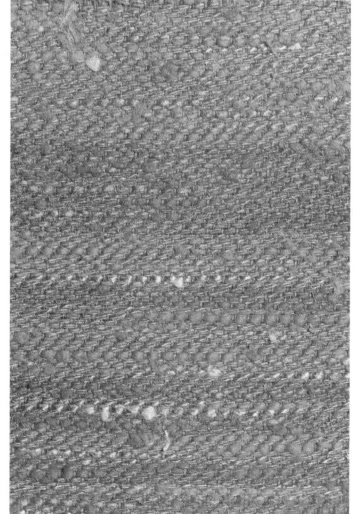

100% Creslan acrylic.
Folker Fabrics Corp.
1964.

Cotton, acetate and rayon upholstery.
Leavitt & Watterston.
1963.

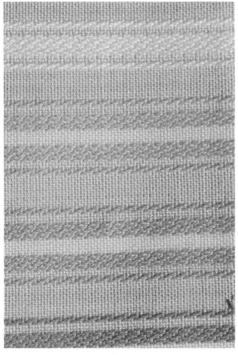 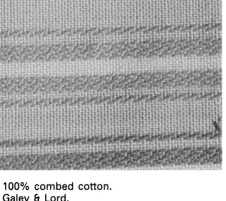 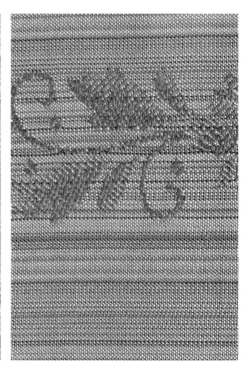

100% combed cotton.
Galey & Lord.
1961.

Cotton and Fortrel polyester.
Klebanow.
1961.

100% silk.
Dai Nippon Spinning Co., Osaka, Japan.
Nichibo, Japan's leading producer of
Textile products.
1961.

100% nylon airplane interior.
Collins & Aikman.
1960.

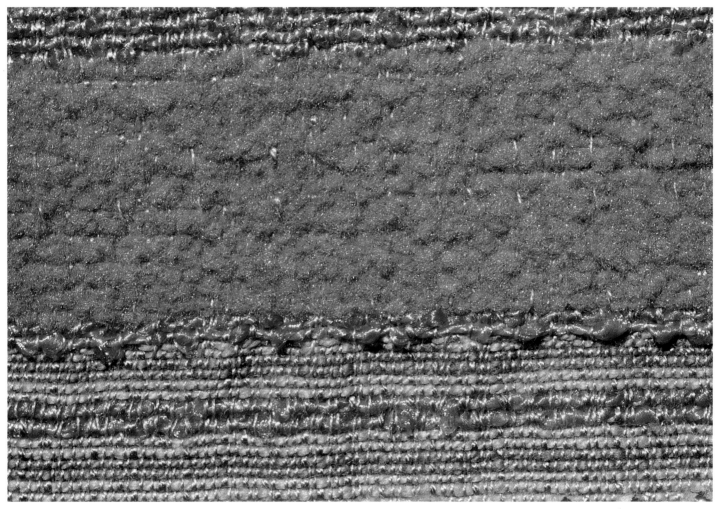

Top left: 100% cotton. Galey & Lord. 1962.

Top right: 100% cotton duck. Avondale. 1961.

Bottom left: 70% rayon, 30% acetate, chiffon velvet stripe. Crompton-Richmond. 1962.

Bottom right: Cotton canvas. Ameritex. 1967.

Top left: 50% Avril, 50% Dacron. Henry Glass. 1969.

Top right: 100% cotton, puckered ribbon stripe. Wamsutta. 1968.

Bottom left: 100% cotton, seersucker. Russell of Alabama. 1961.

Bottom right: 100% cotton, Calcutta stripe. Russell Mills. 1963.

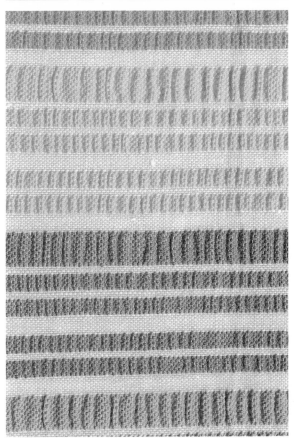

100% Creslan acrylic knit.
Aladdin Knit Mills.
1964.

100% Pima cotton, velour knit.
Security.
1965.

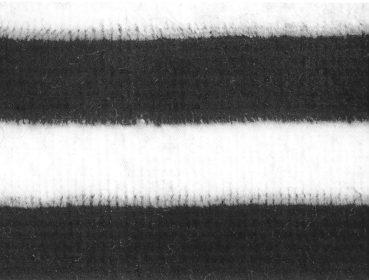

Rayon, acetate, cotton, velvet upholstery.
Collins & Aikman.
1969.

Arnel and rayon.
Cohama.
1966.

Top left: 72% cotton, 28% nylon. Swift Manufacturing Co. 1967.

Top right: Cotton. Cone Mills. 1967.

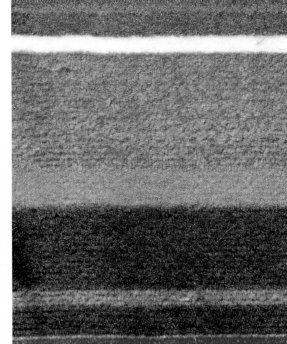

Bottom left: 100% wool Peruvian rug adaptation for Jack Winter. Crestwood. 1960.

Bottom right: Suede denim. Cone Mills. 1967.

Fortrel, cotton.
Galey & Lord.
1966.

Cotton, Glo Glo prints with luminescent pigment.
Old Deerfield Fabrics.
1966.

100% Wool.
Late 1960s.

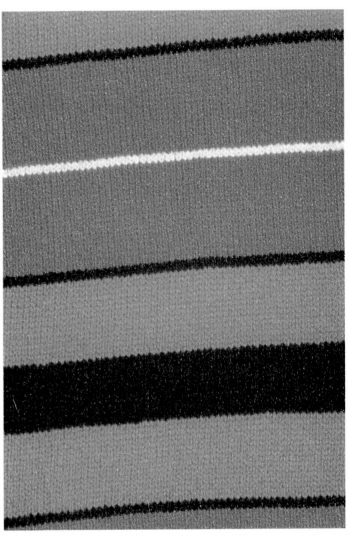

Nylon, Dacron knit stripe .
Stretchnit.
1968.

Dacron and nylon.
Stretchnit.
1967.

Cotton knit.
Alamac Knitting Mills.
1965.

Polyester blend.
Interchem.
1966.

100% nylon knit.
Stretchnit, Inc.
1968.

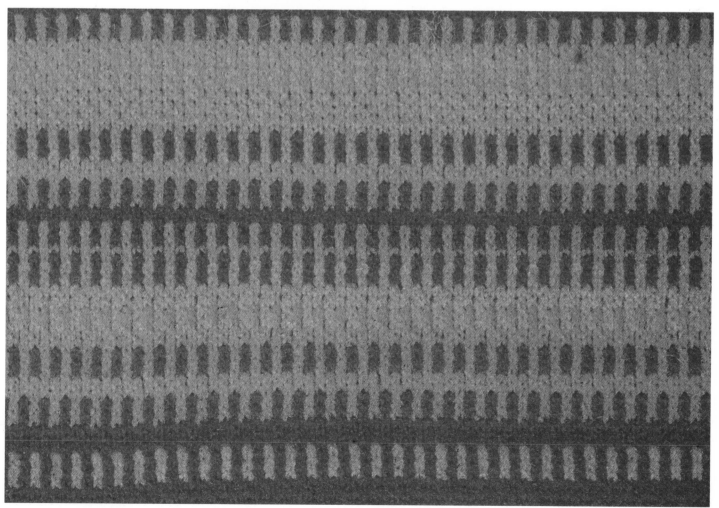

"Toostripe" by Alexander Girard for
Herman Miller.
Orinoka.
1965.

CHAPTER 5

CHECKS & PLAIDS

Top left: Dacron and cotton blend.
Galey & Lord.
1960.

Bottom left: 70% wool, 30% acrylic, Glen plaid pattern.
Milliken Woolens.
1960.

Top right: 94% cotton, 6% Lycra spandex.
DuPont.
1966.

Bottom right: Nylon, stretch denim.
Cone Mills, Inc.
1964.

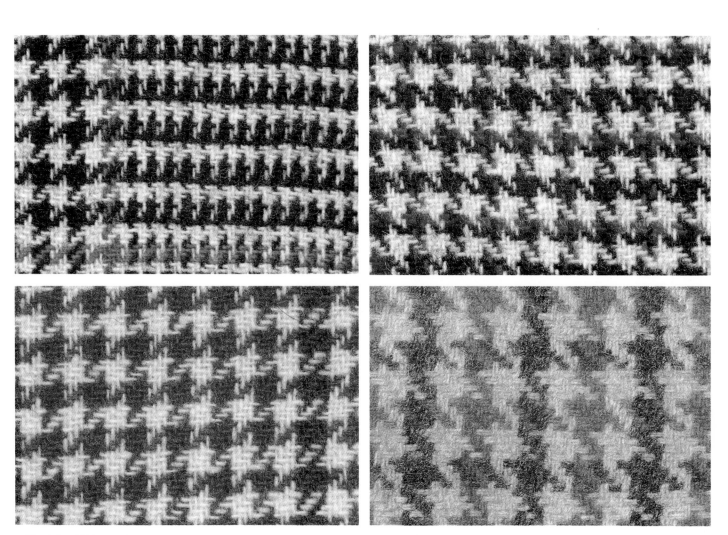

Top left: 100% wool.
The Benvenue.
Guilford.
1962.

Bottom left: 100% wool.
The Prince of Wales.
Guilford.
1962.

Top right: 100% wool.
The Benalder.
Guilford.
1962.

Bottom right: 100% wool, classic check.
Kent Manufacturing.
1962.

100% wool.
Late 1960s.

100% wool hound's-tooth.
Eastland.
1965.

Woven acrylic tweed bonded to acetate tricot.
Wamsutta.
1967.

Top left: Rayon and acetate.
Stevens.
1968.

Bottom left: 100% wool.
The Glenmorriston.
Guilford.
1962.

Top right: 49% rayon, 31% acrylic, 27% polyester, 4% acetate, 4%
Enkrome rayon.
Stevens.
1968.

Bottom right: 100% wool.
The Lochmore.
Guilford.
1962.

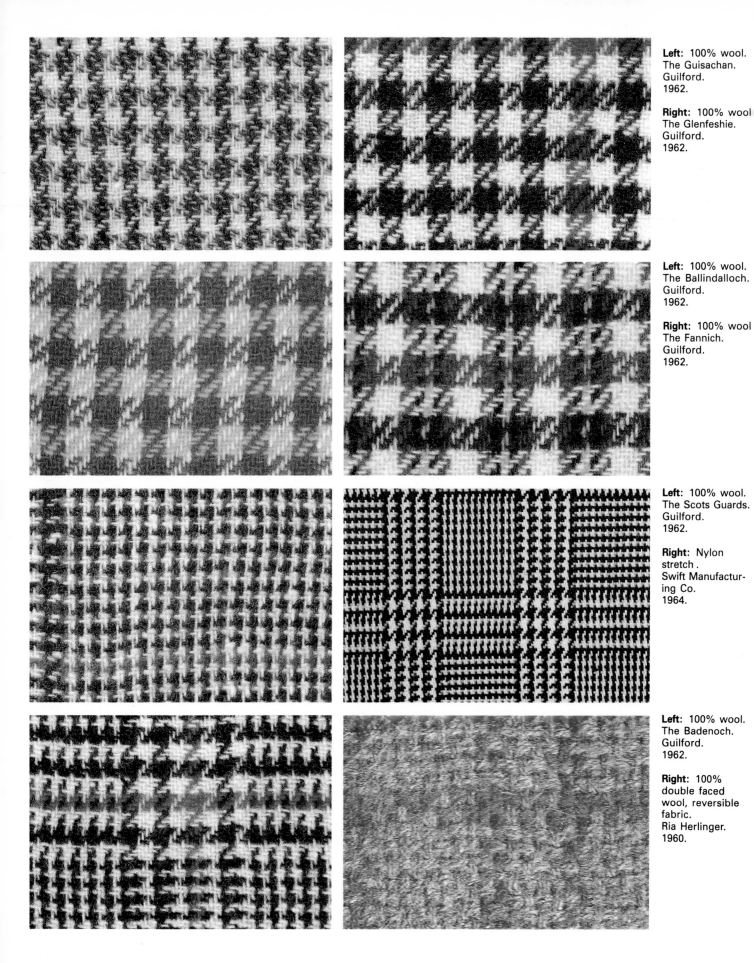

Left: 100% wool.
The Guisachan.
Guilford.
1962.

Right: 100% wool
The Glenfeshie.
Guilford.
1962.

Left: 100% wool.
The Ballindalloch.
Guilford.
1962.

Right: 100% wool
The Fannich.
Guilford.
1962.

Left: 100% wool.
The Scots Guards.
Guilford.
1962.

Right: Nylon
stretch .
Swift Manufactur-
ing Co.
1964.

Left: 100% wool.
The Badenoch.
Guilford.
1962.

Right: 100%
double faced
wool, reversible
fabric.
Ria Herlinger.
1960.

Top left: 100% cotton.
Morgan-Jones Inc.
1960.

Center left: 100% wool.
Late 1960s.

Bottom left: Wool, angora.
Late 1960s.

Top right: Dacron and Avron.
Russell Mfg. Co.
1963.

Center right: 100% cotton, wash-wear finish, Ombre design.
J.P. Stevens.
1961.

Bottom right: 100% cotton.
Galey & Lord.
1962.

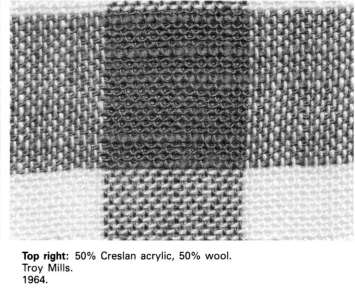

Top left: 100% cotton.
Galey & Lord, a Division of Burlington Industries.
1960.

Bottom left: 50% Creslan acrylic, 50% rayon.
Cohama Fabrics.
1963.

Top right: 50% Creslan acrylic, 50% wool.
Troy Mills.
1964.

Bottom right: Rayon/acetate.
Cohama.
1967.

Top left: 100% Antron nylon taffeta.
Travis Fabrics.
1965.

Bottom left: 50% Arnel tri-acetate, 50% rayon.
Shirley Fabrics by U.S. Royal.
1960.

Top right: 100% Creslan acrylic fiber.
Troy Mills.
1965.

Bottom right: 100% Dacron.
Stehli.
1961.

Cotton yarn-dyed seersucker.
Russell Mills, Inc.
1965.

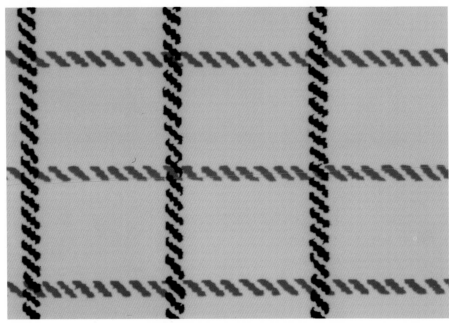

Vinyl.
Comark.
1966.

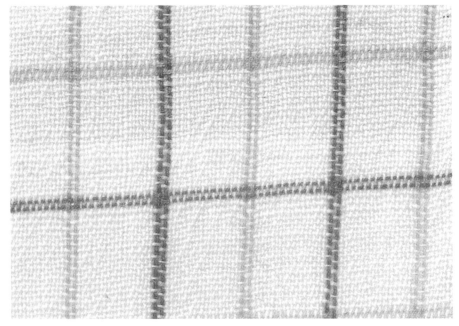

Worsted crepe.
Bristol Fabrics, Ltd.
1964.

100% cotton.
Russell of Alabama.
1962.

100% wool.
Late 1960s.

100% cotton.
Cone Mills.
1963.

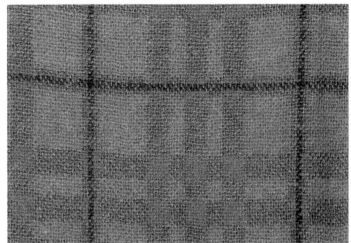

100% Creslan acrylic fiber.
Troy Mills.
1965.

100% Dacron.
Cohama.
1961.

100% cotton broadcloth.
Wamsutta.
1963.

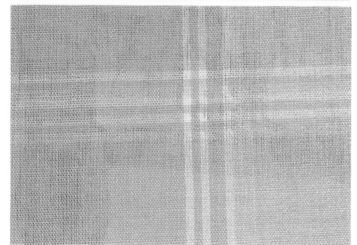

50% Creslan acrylic, 50% rayon.
Franklin.
1961.

Sheer Dacron and cotton plaid.
Galey & Lord.
1961.

50% acrylic, 50% rayon.
U.S. Royal.
1960.

50% Acrilan acrylic, 50% rayon.
U.S. Royal.
1960.

100% cotton madras.
Mission Valley.
1963.

50% acrylic, 50% rayon.
U.S. Royal.
1960.

Opposite page:
Top: Fortrel and combed cotton.
Galey & Lord.
1966.

Bottom: Acetate, rayon, and silk plaid.
Auburn.
1966.

100% cotton.
M. Lowenstein & Sons.
1965.

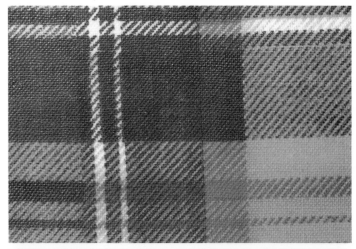

100% silk, India madras inspired.
Auburn.
1960.

50% Creslan acrylic, 50% rayon.
Earl-Loom.
1963.

50% Arnel tri-acetate, 50% rayon.
Shirley Fabrics by U.S. Royal.
1960.

Top left: Rayon, cotton, acetate.
Cohama.
1965.

Center left: 100% Creslan acrylic fiber.
Troy Mills.
1965.

Bottom left: 50-50 blend of Acrilan and wool.
Cyril Johnson.
1960.

Top right: 100% Creslan acrylic fiber.
Troy Mills.
1965.

Center right: 100% wool.
Ria Herlinger Fabrics, Inc.
1960.

Bottom right: 50-50 Acrilan and rayon.
Fabrex.
1960.

35% wool, 65% Orlon, earth color.
Milliken Woolens.
1961.

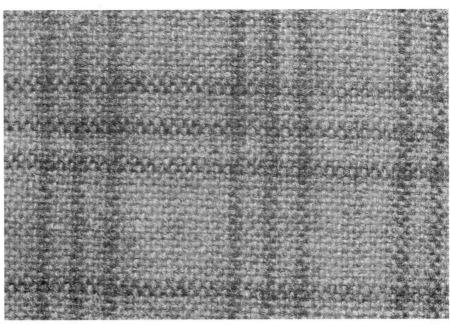

Kaycel printed non-woven.
Butler Paper Co.
1962.

100% wool.
Late 1960s.

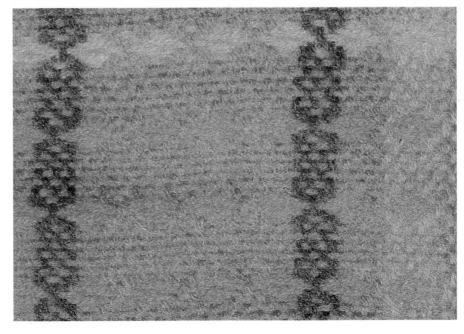

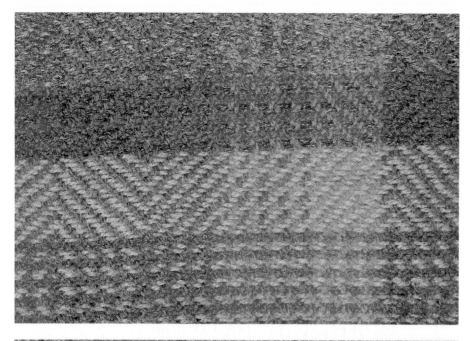

100% wool.
Late 1960s.

50% Creslan acrylic, 50%
Coloray rayon.
Reeves Brothers.
1964.

Arnel and cotton seersucker.
Crestwood Corp.
1963.

Rayon with acrylic.
Blentempo.
1967.

50% Kodel, 40% rayon, 10% flax.
Crown Fabrics.
1965.

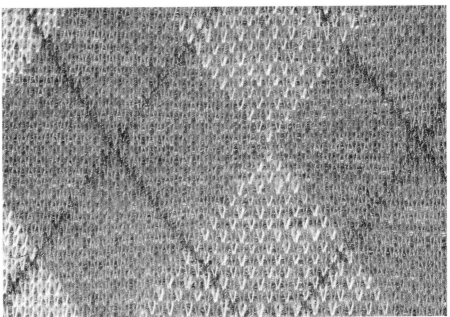

70% Zefran II, 30% Modacrylic bonded to
tricot; miniature argyle.
B & E Mills.
1968.

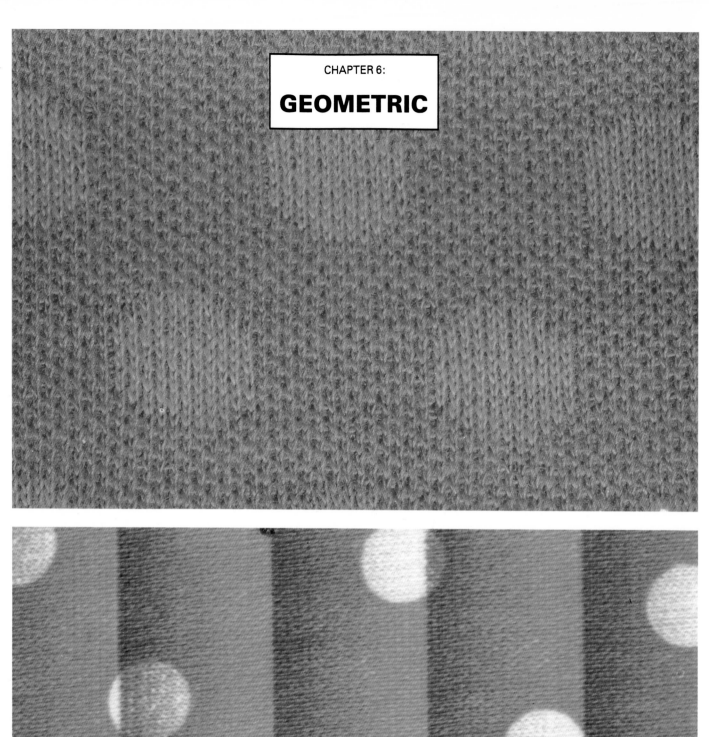

CHAPTER 6:

GEOMETRIC

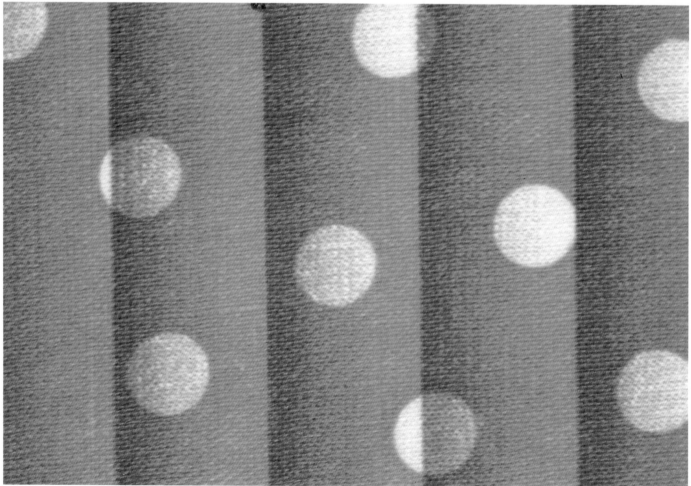

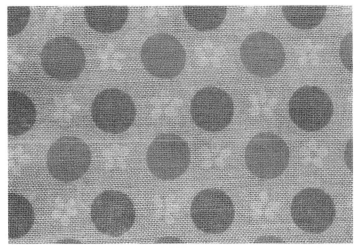

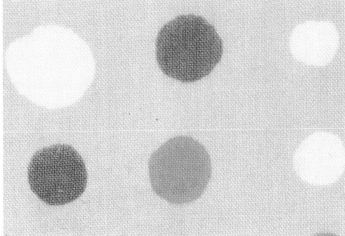

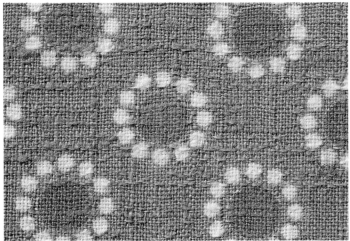

Top left: 100% cotton, Syl-mer finish.
Springs Mills.
1961.

Bottom left: 50/50 Fortrel, polyester, cotton.
Rosewood Fabrics.
1965.

Top right: 80% Dacron polyester, 20% cotton.
Klopman.
1964.

Bottom right: 100% cotton.
Cone Mills.
1960.

Opposite page:
Top: Cotton knit.
Ware Knitters.
1965.

Bottom: 100% cotton, Trompe l'Oeil print.
M. Lowenstein & Sons.
1968.

Synthetic stretch knit.
1969.

Kaycel paper dress, throwaway clothes.
Kimberly-Stevens.
1966.

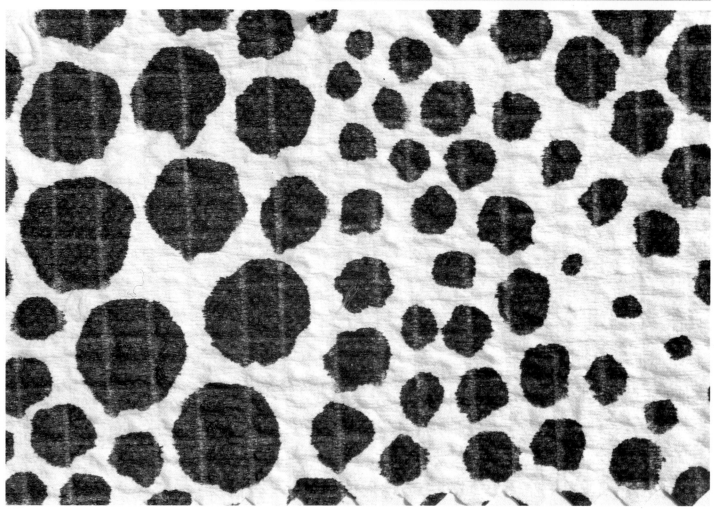

Avril, polyester.
Berkshire-Hathaway.
1969.

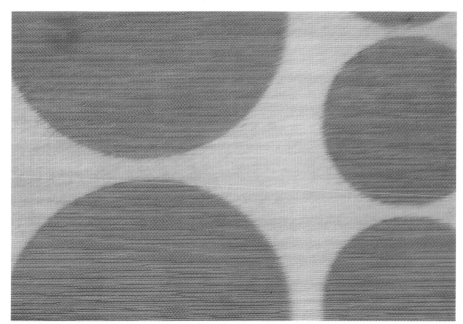

Cotton satin.
Cranston.
1964.

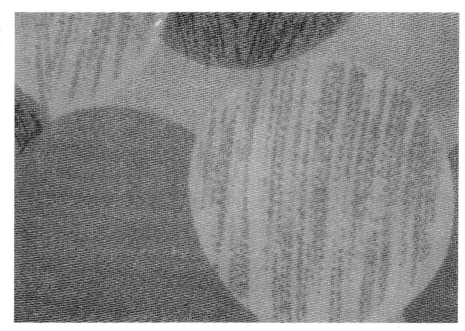

Arnel triacetate by Celanese.
Stehli & Co.
1965.

100% wool challis.
Romique Fabrics.
1964.

100% cotton tapestry weave.
Quality Looms.
1960.

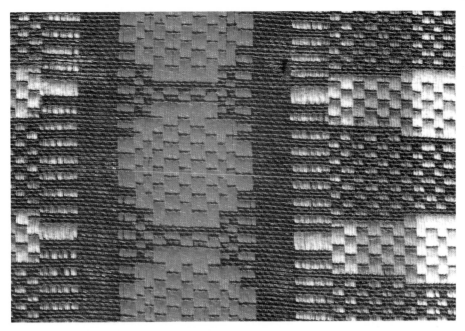

80% stretch nylon, 20% polyester knit.
Stretch Fabrics, Inc.
1965.

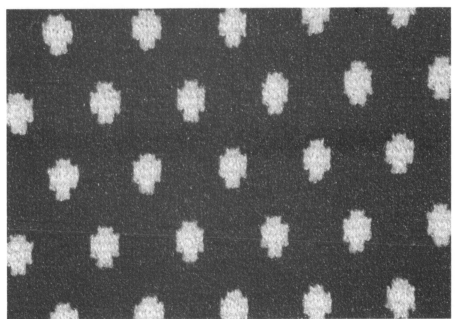

100% Pima cotton print.
Wamsutta.
1963.

53% cotton, 47% polyurethane, Op Art.
Prentiss-Lane Inc.
1965.

100% nylon, Op Art.
Prentiss-Lane Inc.
1965.

100% nylon, Op Art.
Prentiss-Lane Inc.
1965.

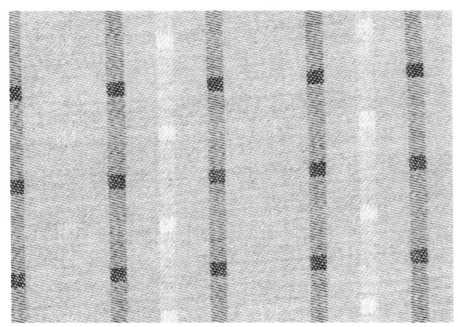

100% wool.
Late 1960s.

Synthetic knit.
1969.

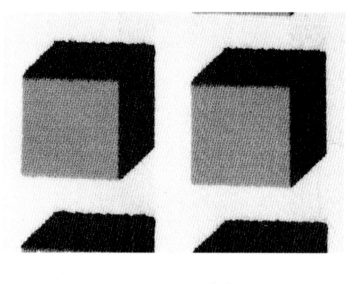

Synthetic knit.
1969.

Top: 50% Kodel, 50% Avril; psychedelic.
Horizon Fabrics.
1967.

Bottom: 100% cotton; source of inspiration was Westerfield
Collection at the Ford Museum, Dearborn, Michigan.
Greeff.
1960.

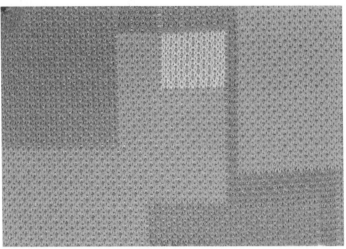

Top left: Dacron polyester, yarn dye.
DuPont.
1967.

Top right: Dacron polyester, print.
DuPont.
1967.

Bottom left: 100% silk print.
Stehli.
1961.

Bottom right: Arnel triacetate.
Prentiss-Lane.
1965.

100% wool.
Late 1960s.

Fortrel doubleknit chevrons.
B & E Mills.
1968.

Opposite page:
Top: 100% wool.
Ria Herlinger.
1967.

Bottom: 100% Dacron.
Deering Milliken.
1967.

100% cotton, Aztec print.
Avondale.
1966.

95% Celanese acetate, 5% nylon.
Mil-Art.
1966.

95% Acetate, 5% nylon.
Mil-Art, Inc.
1968.

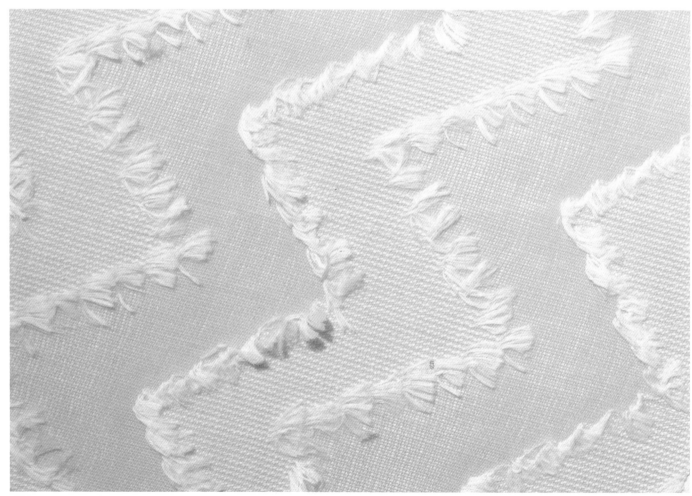

100% cotton bonded to Celanese acetate-tricot knit; geometric Inca pattern.
Abaco.
1967.

100% woven cotton, peasant handicrafts inspired.
Exclusive.
1961.

Opposite page:
Top: "Barber Pole" by Alexander Girard for Herman Miller.
American Art.
1961.

Bottom: 65% Dacron, polyester, 35% cotton eyelash voile.
Wamsutta.
1968.

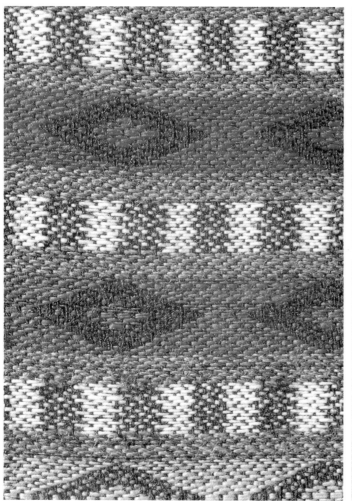

50/50 blend of Acrilan and rayon, Syl-mer finish.
Milliken.
1961.

Top right: 100% wool.
Late 1960s.

Bottom right: Dacron and cotton blend, made
especially for Pauline Trigére, Greek influence.
Galey & Lord.
1960.

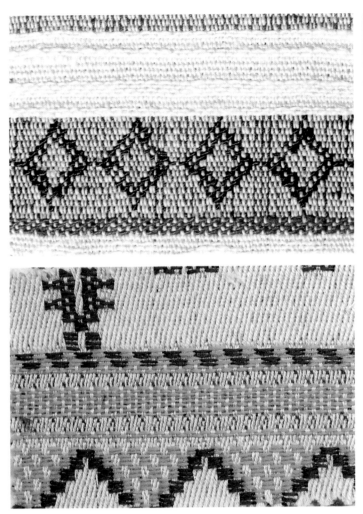

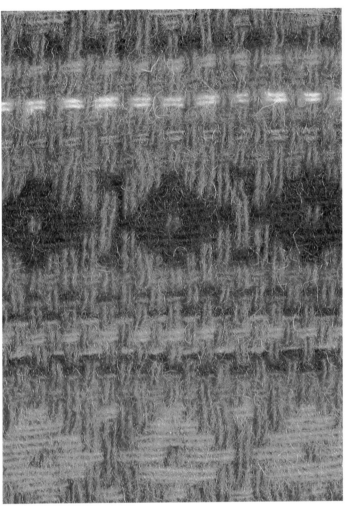

Top left: 100% cotton by Penco, Syl-mer finish.
Burlington House.
1961.

Bottom left: 63% rayon, 37% cotton upholstery cloth.
Boris Kroll.
1969.

100% wool.
Amana Woolens.
1968.

100% cotton tapestry.
Cohama.
1960.

100% cotton corduroy print.
Crompton-Richmond Co.
1966.

104

Top left: Cotton and Dacron; African inspired.
Alamac.
Mid 1960s.

Bottom left: Wool.
Early 1960s.

Top right: 100% wool jacquard stripe, Angus Park woolen.
Deerfield.
1960.

Bottom right: Foam laminated knit, Bondaknit Fabric.
Abaco.
1961.

100% cotton print.
Fuller.
1960.

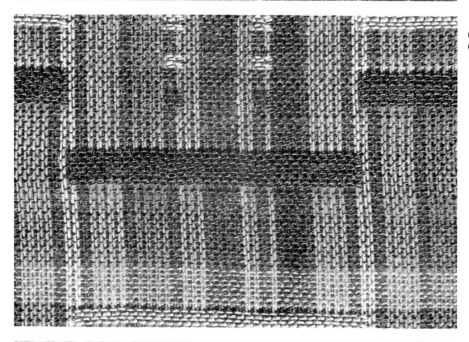

Cotton and Dacron, African inspired.
Galey & Lord.
1961.

100% wool worsted double knit.
Deering Milliken.
1961.

Opposite page:
Top: 100% Dacron, Art Deco
revival.
Originit.
1969.

Bottom: 100% wool worsted,
geometric design.
Anglo Fabrics.
1968.

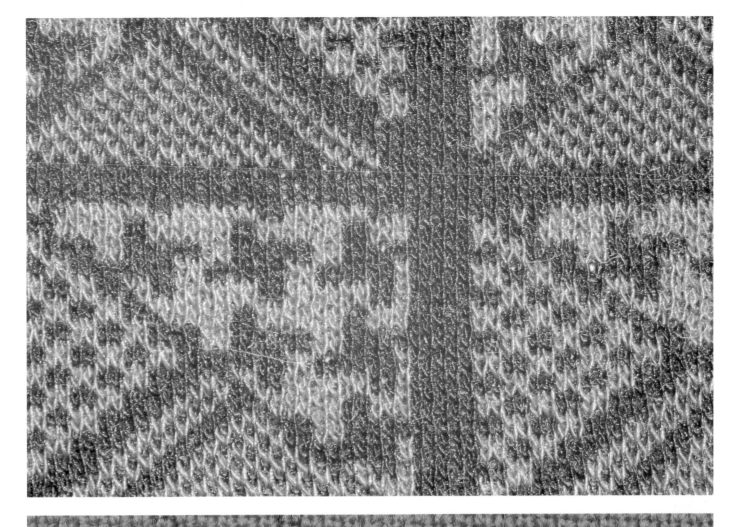

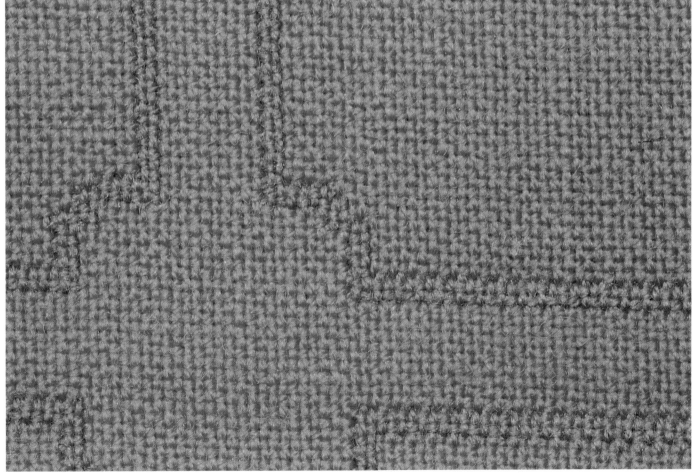

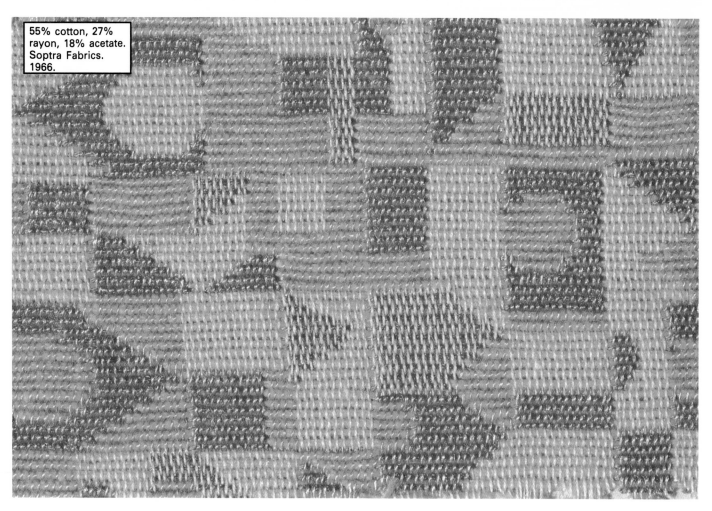

55% cotton, 27% rayon, 18% acetate. Soptra Fabrics. 1966.

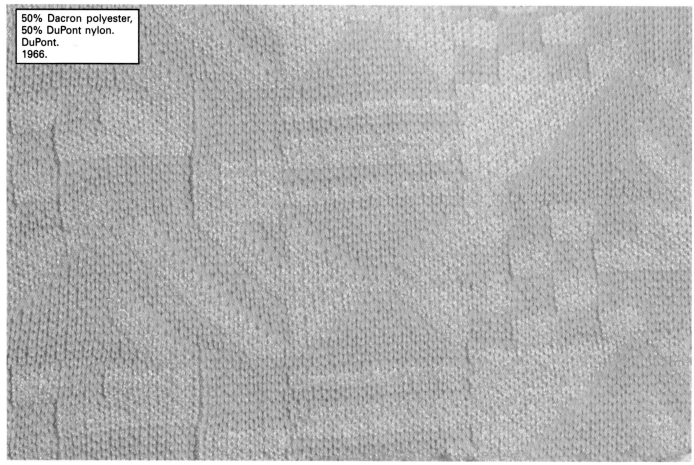

50% Dacron polyester, 50% DuPont nylon. DuPont. 1966.

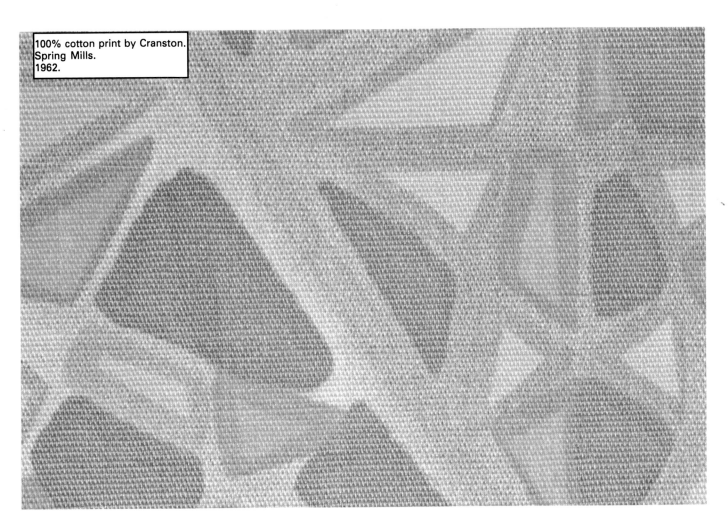

100% cotton print by Cranston.
Spring Mills.
1962.

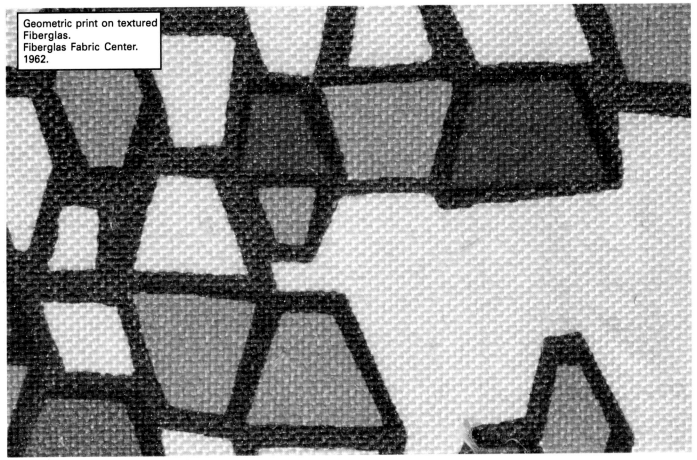

Geometric print on textured
Fiberglas.
Fiberglas Fabric Center.
1962.

Top left: 100% Dacron polyester challis.
DuPont.
1965.

Top right: Caprolan nylon, fabric used by Oscar de la Renta, printed by Carjer Looms.
Allied Chemical.
1967.

Left: Poly blend.
Interchem.
1966.

Lifebond color blend.
Hilton-Davis Chemical Co.
1967.

Top right: Heat transfer design.
Sublistatic Corp.
1968.

Bottom right: Arnel jersey, geometric.
Wamsutta.
1968.

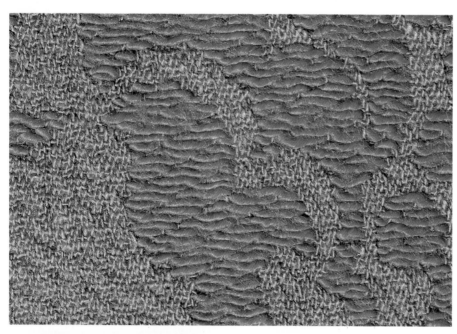

CHAPTER 7

ABSTRACT

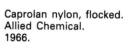

Caprolan nylon, flocked.
Allied Chemical.
1966.

100% cotton.
Bates.
1965.

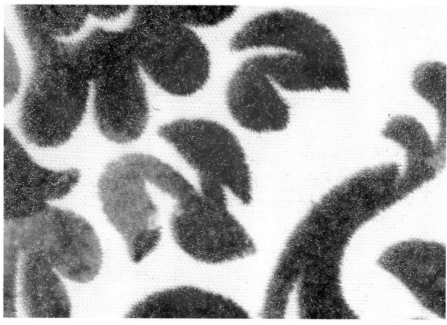

Dacron, sheer batiste.
Milton H. Stern Associates.
1966.

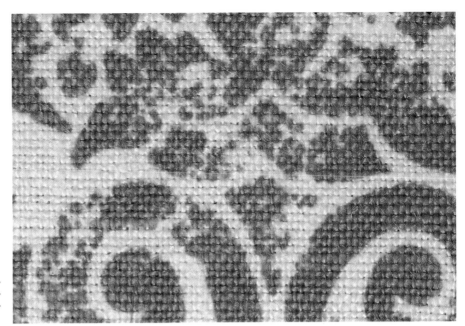

100% Belgian linen, Spanish inspired.
Belmont by F. Schumacher.
1961.

Cotton.
Everfast.
1964.

Fiberglas bouclé print.
Schumacher.
1962.

100% stretch nylon.
Edmos Sales Co.
1967.

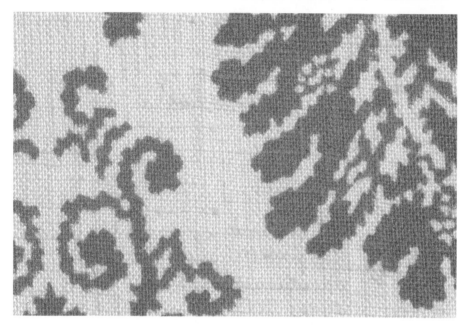

50% Kodel, 50% cotton.
Everfast.
1966.

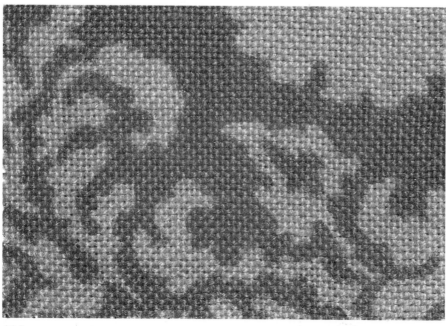

Cotton.
Everfast.
1964.

Opposite page:
Top: Cotton.
Everfast.
1964.

Bottom: Cotton.
Everfast.
1964.

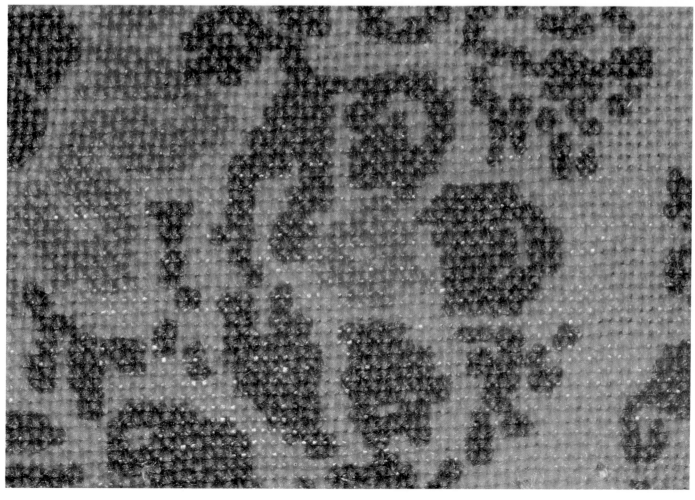

Nu-jute fabric, Sundra.
Everfast.
1967.

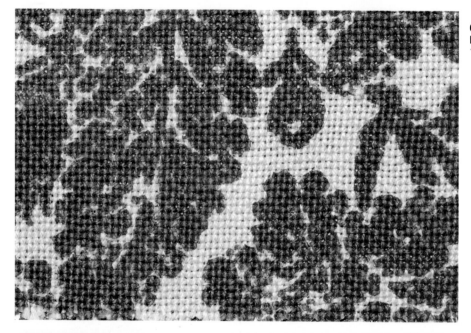

Cotton.
Everfast.
1964.

100% combed cotton upholstery.
Everfast.
1961.

Oppostie page:
Top: Vinyl.
Tiger Fabrics.
1966.

Bottom: 100% Arnel
triacetate, Ondeze print.
Cohama.
1966.

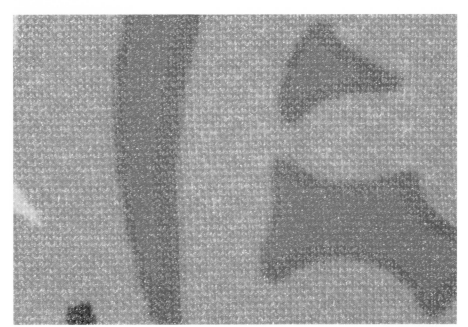

The first printed Ban-Lon doubleknit, DuPont nylon, design by H.M. Kolbe.
Armtex, Inc.
1967.

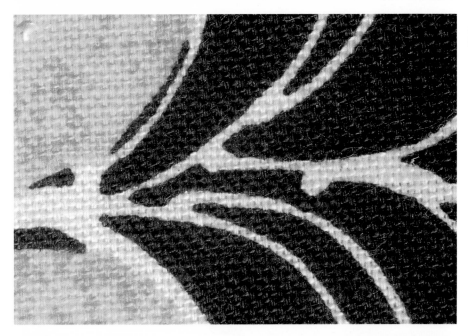

Cotton print.
Everfast.
1968.

100% silk.
Emilio Pucci.
1960.

Opposite page:
Top: Cotton velveteen, Persian medallion design.
Crompton-Richmond.
1968.

Bottom: Double knit nylon.
Blue Ridge-Winkler.
1966.

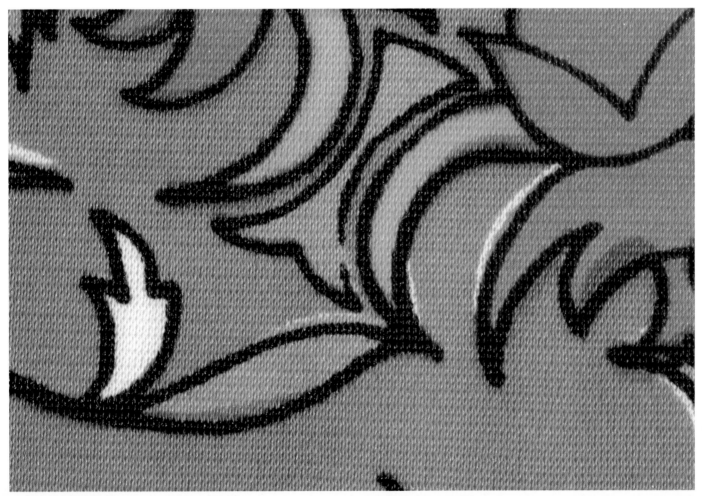

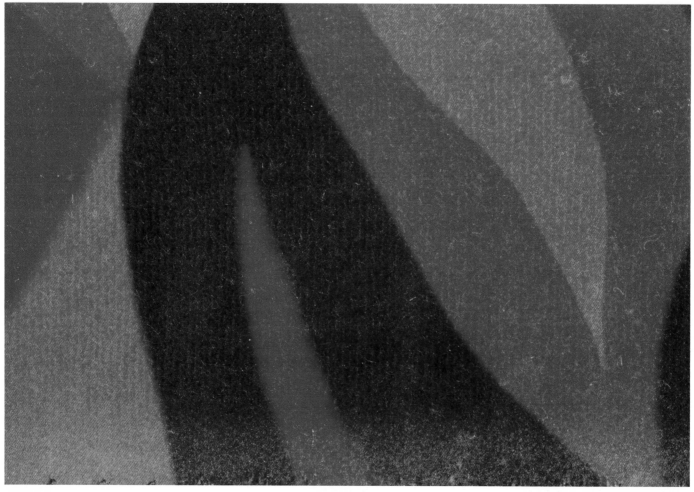

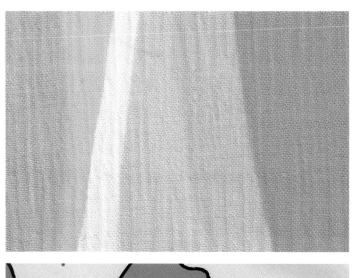

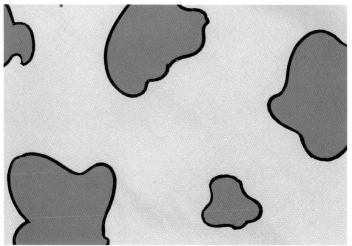

Top left: 100% Pima cotton crinkle crepe.
William Anderson Textiles.
1966.

Bottom left: Silk.
Mid 1960s.

Top right: 65% Fortrel, 35% Avril blend.
Wamsutta.
1964.

Bottom right: 100% Caprolan nylon.
Fabritique.
1965.

Opposite page:
Top: 100% cotton.
Bancroft.
1968.

Bottom: Cotton velveteen.
Crompton-Richmond.
1968.

Rayon, acetate print.
Chardon-Marche.
1969.

100% Orlon.
Cortley Fabrics.
1966.

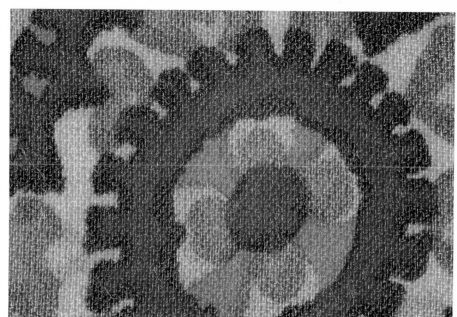

65% Dacron, 35% rayon.
Rosewood.
1965.

Blended cotton and flax.
Cone Mills.
1960.

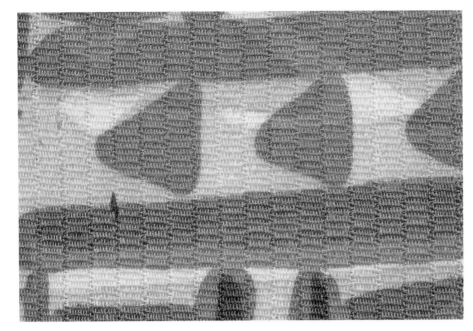

100% cotton, batik inspired.
Avondale.
1960.

Polyester blend.
Interchem.
1966.

100% Dacron batiste.
Goodman & Theise.
1961.

Celanese rayon and acetate, drapery design.
Covington.
1961.

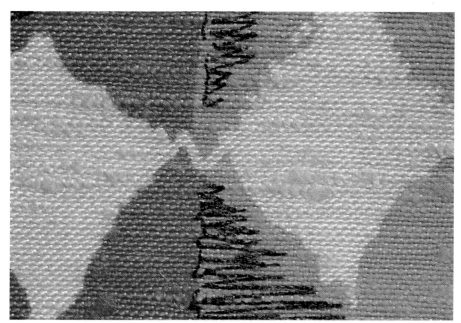

50% Vycron, 50% rayon printed voile.
Frankly.
1961.

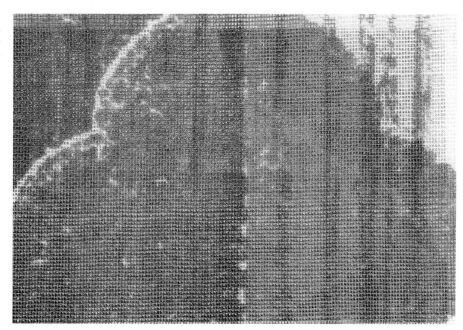

100% cotton knit.
Concord.
1962.

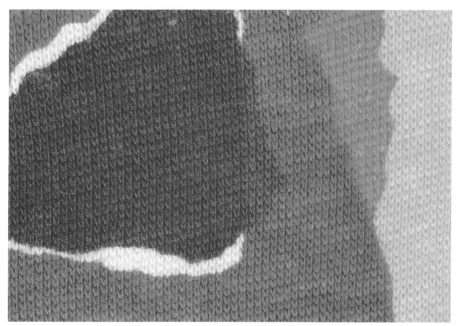

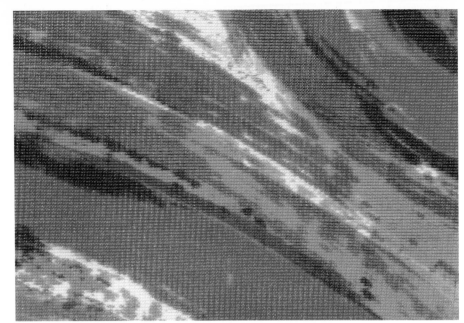

Caprolan nylon.
Fiesta Fabrics, Inc.
1964.

Caprolan nylon.
Fiesta Fabrics, Inc.
1964.

Polyester nonwoven.
DHJ Industries Inc.
1967.

100% cotton, batik inspired .
Roberson Associates.
1960.

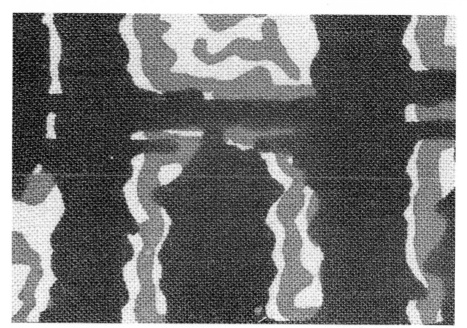

100% cotton, batik inspired.
Fuller Fabrics.
1960.

100% cotton, abstract floral.
Signature Fabrics.
1961.

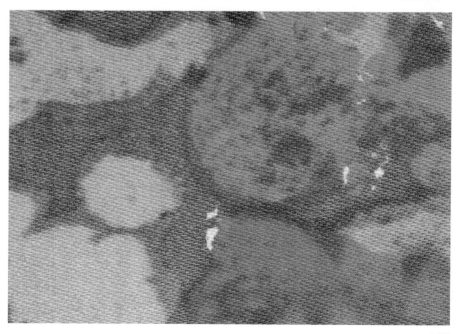

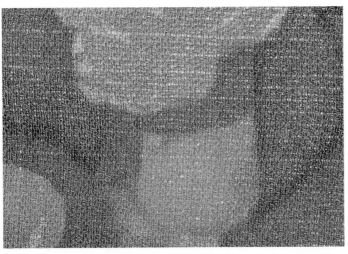

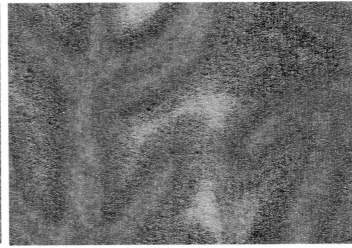

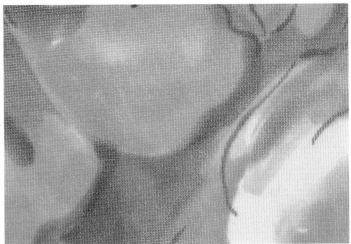

Top left: 50% Avril, 50% Arnel.
Rosewood.
1963.

Bottom left: 100% Creslan challis.
Robaix.
1962.

Top right: Nylon velour by Palthe.
Enka.
1962.

Bottom right: Caprolan 30 denier nylon.
Robaix.
1966.

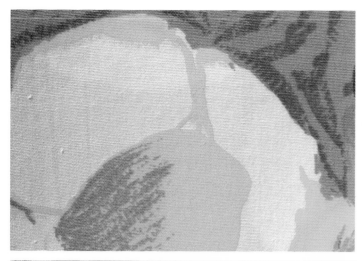

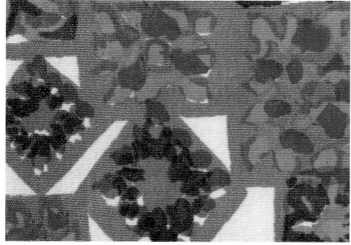

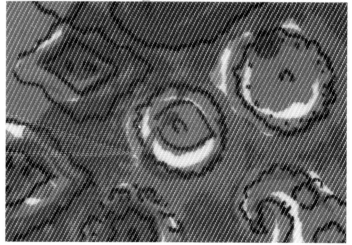

Top left: 100% Supima cotton sateen, Hawaiian inspired, designed by Harvey Seltzer of Westport Fabrics in cooperation with the Cranston Screen Print Division.
Cranston.
1961.

Bottom left: 100% Supima cotton, "Temple of the Dawn," Thailand print.
Cranston.
1961.

Top right: 100% cotton, India madras inspired, designed by Alice Papazian.
Concord.
1961.

Bottom right: 100% Arnel, Persian inspired.
Joyce.
1961.

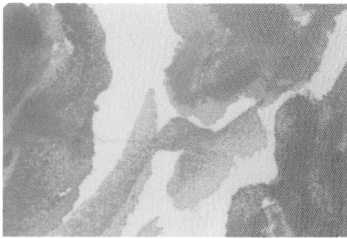

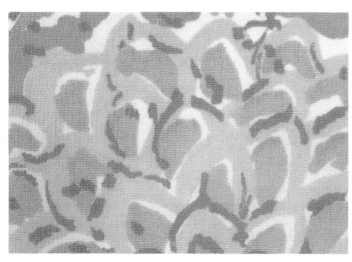

Top left: Durst longcloth.
Bangor Mills, a Division of Collins & Aikman.
1963.

Bottom left: Kodel cotton print.
Everfast.
1963.

Top right: Fortrel polyester.
Travis.
1965.

Bottom right: Caprolan nylon.
Prentiss-Lane Inc.
1965.

Opposite page:
Top left: 65% Dacron polyester, 35% cotton.
DuPont.
1965.

Top right: Kodel cotton print.
Everfast.
1963.

Bottom: 100% cotton.
Everfast.
1961.

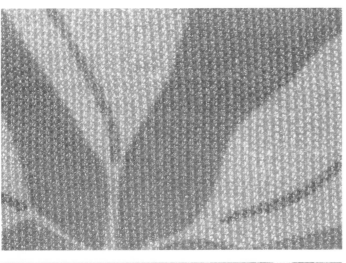

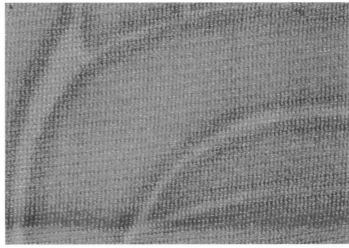

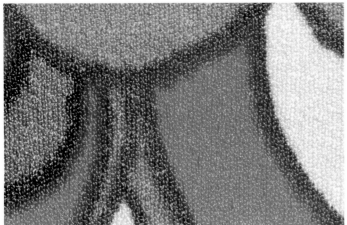

Top left: Enkalure nylon.
William Winkler Inc.
1965.

Bottom left: 100% textured nylon.
Brauer.
1966.

Top right: Caprolan nylon stretch knit.
Donson Fabrics.
1966.

Bottom right: 100% wool crepe.
Berman.
1963.

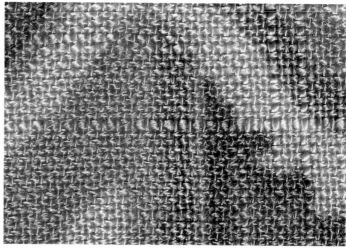

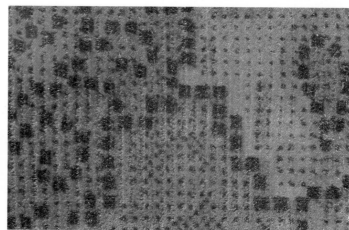

Top left: 100% wool print, basket weave.
Cohama.
1963.

Bottom left: Polyester.
J & G Knits.
1969.

Top right: Viscose spun rayon.
Boussac of France.
1964.

Bottom right: 100% cotton pinwale corduroy, motif derived from gros point embroidery.
Cone.
1961.

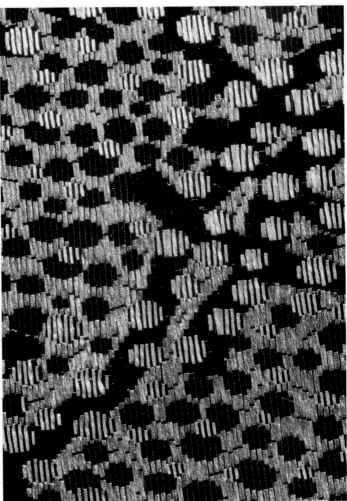

Top left: 100% Zefkrome.
Roma Knit Division of Crown Fabrics.
1963.

Bottom left: 100% cotton, hopsacking print.
Lowenstein & Sons.
1960.

Lacquered rayon imported from Bucol in Paris, tortoise shell
pattern, rainwear.
Lawrence of London.
1960.

Top left: 100% linen.
1966.

Bottom left: Kodel, cotton print.
Everfast.
1963.

Top right: Dacron wash-wear, wrinkle-resistant .
Fabrics by Joyce.
1960.

Bottom right: 100% cotton denim.
Swift Textiles Inc.
1969.

100% silk.
Mid 1960s.

Kodel, cotton.
Everfast.
1963.

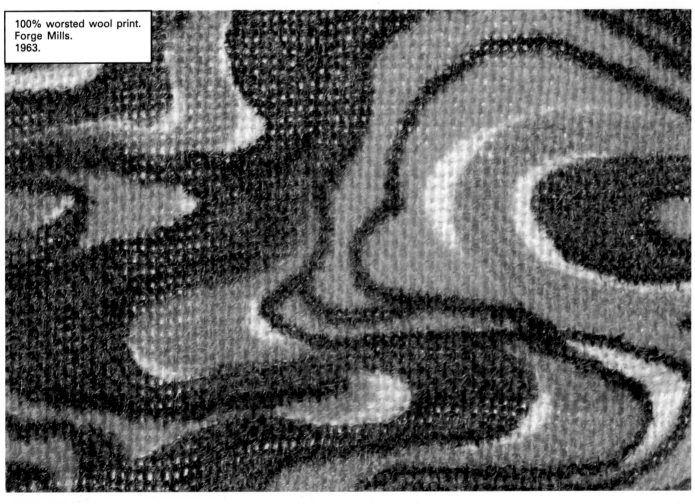

100% worsted wool print.
Forge Mills.
1963.

100% silk.
Mid 1960s.

100% cotton.
Late 1960s.

100% cotton.
Late 1960s.

100% cotton.
Late 1960s.

100% cotton knit, hand tie-dye.
Late 1960s.

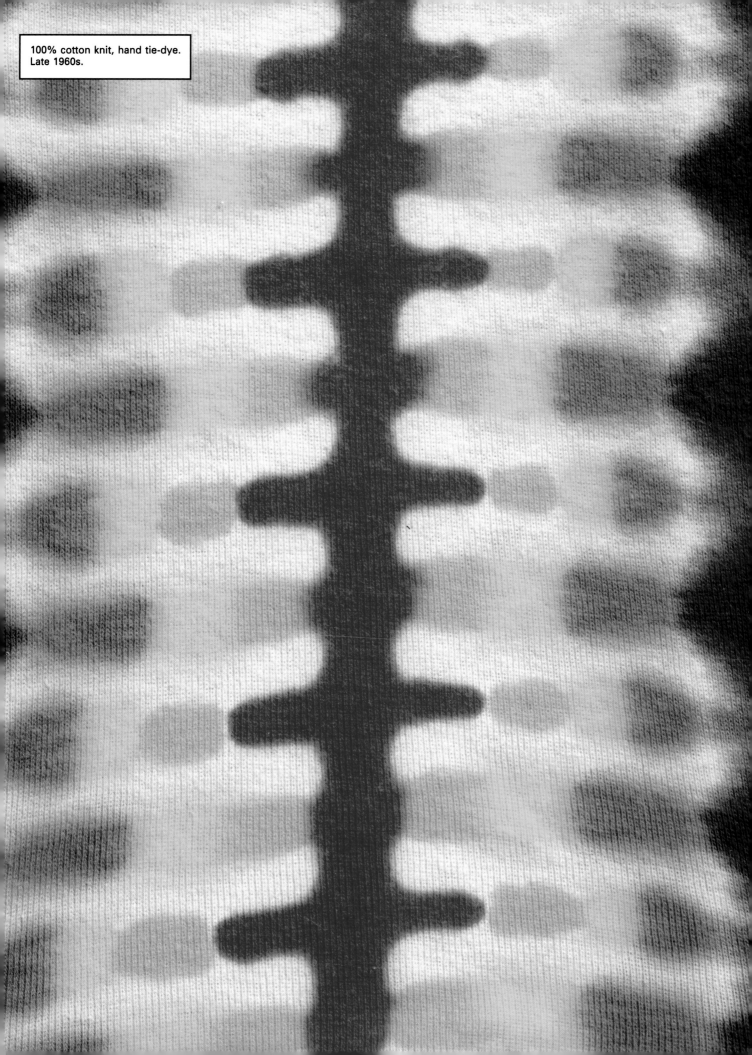

100% cotton knit, hand tie-dye.
Late 1960s.

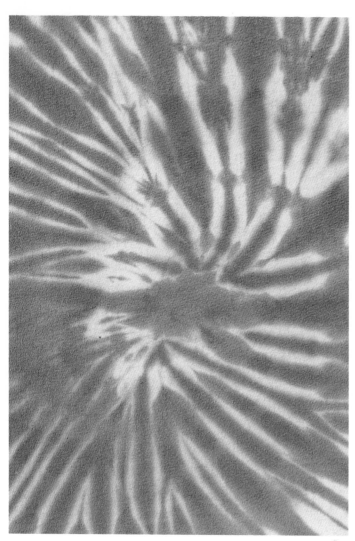

100% cotton knit, hand tie-dye.
Late 1960s.

100% cotton knit, hand tie-dye.
Late 1960s.

100% silk warp print.
A.P. Silk Co.
1960.

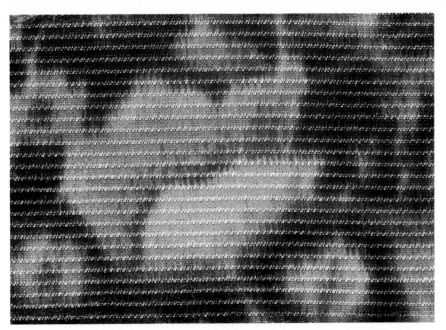

100% silk warp print.
Ottoman.
Shamash.
1960.

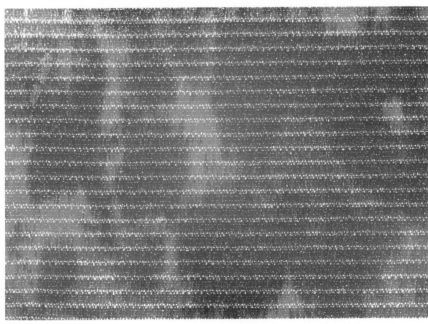

Design by Belding-Corticelli; printing by
Allied Textile Printers.
1960.

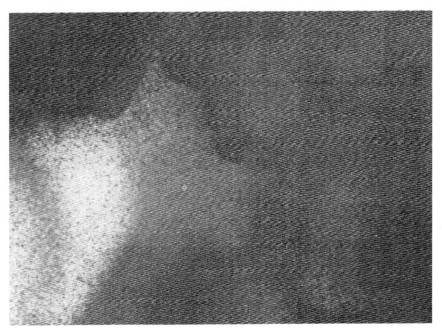

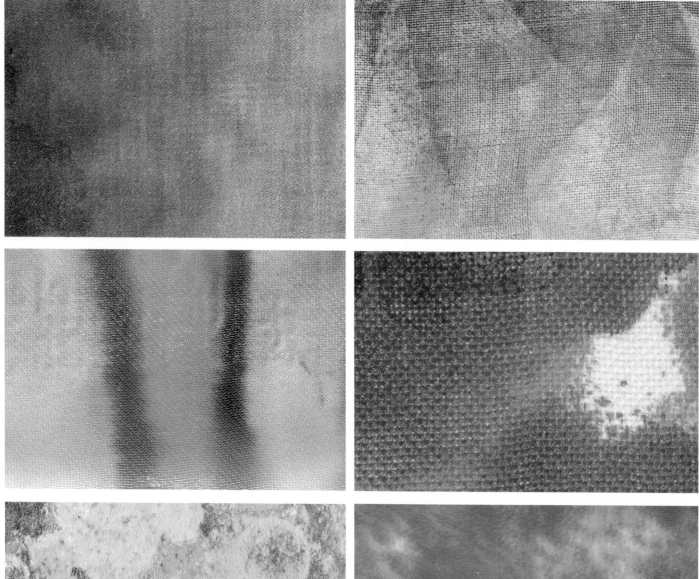

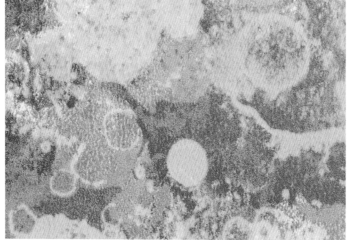

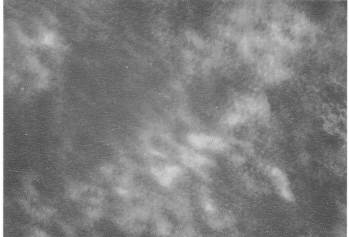

Top left: Design by Belding-Corticelli; printing by Allied Textile Printers.
1960.

Center left: 100% nylon.
G. Hirsch & Sons.
1968.

Bottom left: Caribe, patent leather vinyl.
Comark.
1966.

Top right: 100% combed cotton chiffon.
Fuller Fabrics.
1960.

Center right: 100% Creslan acrylic.
Folker Fabrics Corp.
1964.

Bottom right: Vinyl.
Comark.
1966.

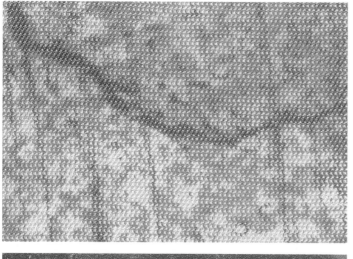

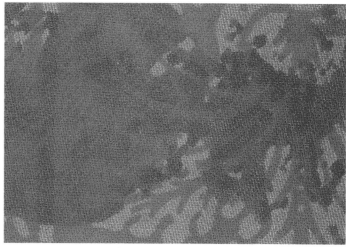

Top left: Nylon and Arnel.
Joyce.
1965.

Center left: Velveteen.
Fabric by Lawrence of London; stained glass design printed by
Menke Lieberman.
Crompton-Richmond.
1960.

Bottom left: Corduroy.
Cone Mills.
1969.

Top right: 50% cotton, 50% Avril.
Cohama.
1965.

Center right: 65% Dacron, 35% rayon blend.
Lowenstein.
1961.

Bottom right: Corfam.
Belle Fabrics.
1967.

CHAPTER 8

FLORAL

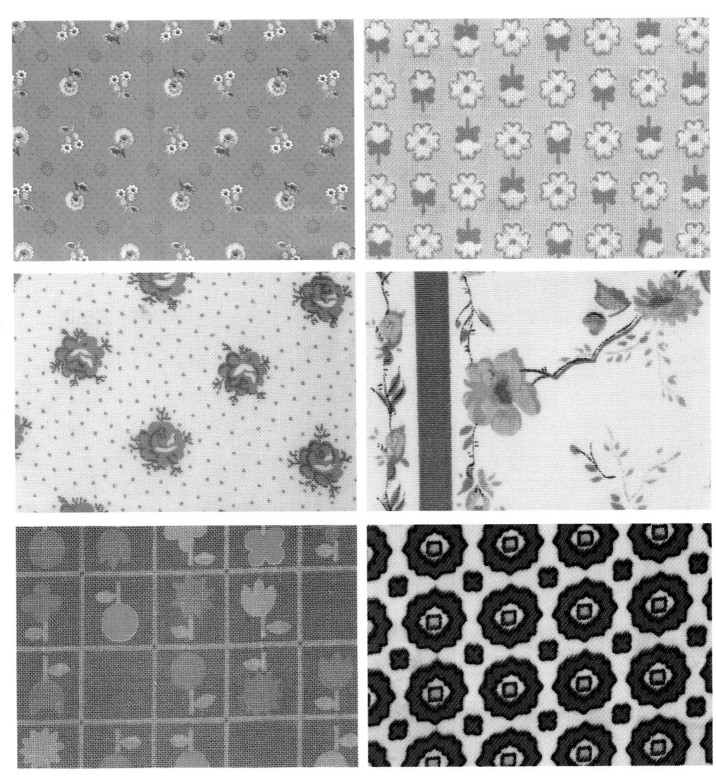

Top left: 100% cotton.
early 1960s.

Center left: 100% combed
cotton.
Brookhaven Textile Co.
1965.

Bottom left: 100% cotton.
A.B.C.
1962.

Top right: 100% cotton.
Converse & Co.
1962.

Center right: 65% Dacron, 35%
Avril rayon.
Wamsutta.
1963.

Bottom right: Antron, new
nylon fiber developed by
DuPont .
Goodman & Theise.
1960.

100% combed cotton print, miniature floral,
American inspired.
Cortley.
1961.

Cotton knit.
Tiger Fabrics.
1965.

100% silk with metallic.
Hirsch Sons, Inc.
1960.

60% combed cotton,
40% Helanca nylon,
stretch fabric.
Stretch Fabrics.
1961.

68% rayon, 32% stretch
nylon.
New England Textile.
1966.

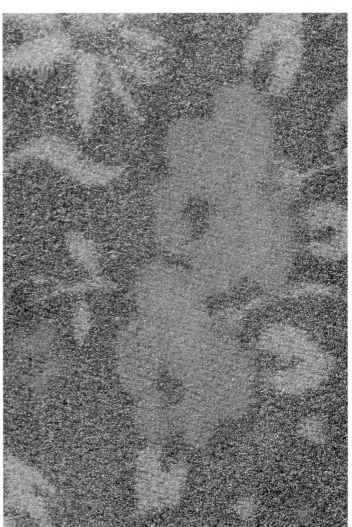

100% cotton, floral print.
Lowenstein.
1961.

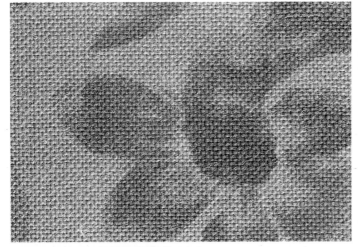

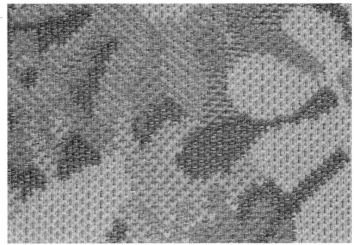

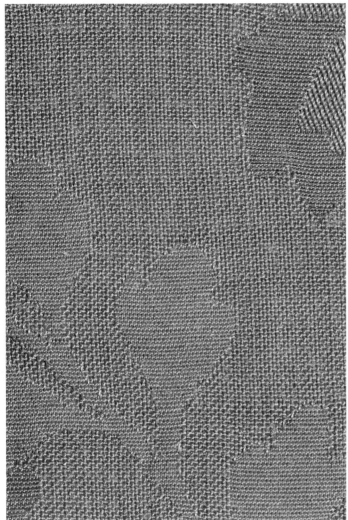

Tapestry knit in Crimplene.
British Import Knit.
1968.

Opposite page:
Top left: 100% cotton upholstery velvet.
Bates.
1965.

Top right: Arnel jersey.
Wamsutta.
1968.

100% cotton.
Bates.
1965.

Bottom: 100% Touch nylon.
J.P. Stevens & Co.
1969.

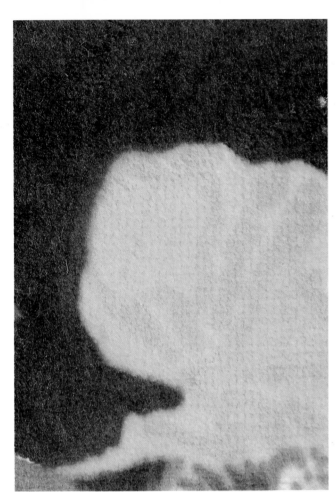

Top left: 100% silk. Scalamandre Silks. 1960.

Top right: 65% Dacron, 35% cotton. Travis. 1965.

Bottom left: 100% Zontrel. Cranston Print Works. Waldburger. 1961.

Bottom right: Cotton roller print. Everfast. 1966.

Top left: 100%
linen print,
designed by Vera
for F. Schumacher;
Greek inspired.
F. Schumacher Co.
1960.

Top right: 100%
cotton, damask
pattern.
Everfast.
1960.

Bottom left: 100%
Creslan acrylic
fiber.
Loomskill.
1962.

Bottom right:
Avril rayon and
cotton.
Joyce.
1966.

50/50 polyester and combed cotton.
Bates.
1965.

Nylon matte-textured Ban-Lon knit.
Soptra Fabrics.
1965.

Polyester blend.
Interchem.
1966.

Kodel polyester and cotton print.
Everfast.
1963.

152

Polyester blend.
Interchem.
1966.

Cotton daisy and dot print.
Tiger Fabrics.
1965.

Cotton print.
Interchem.
1965.

Kodel polyester and cotton print.
Everfast.
1963.

100% cotton, Japanese inspired print
"Kimono Border".
Pembroke Squires for Cabana.
1961.

50% Avril rayon, 50% cotton.
Ameritex, a Division of Cohn
Hall Marx.
1962.

100% cotton.
Late 1960s.

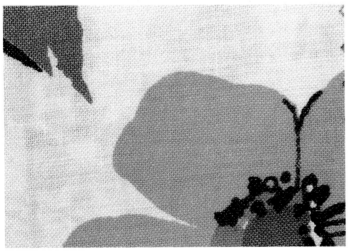

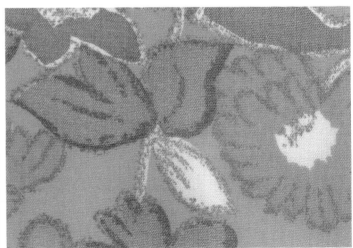

Top left: Avil/cotton blend.
Schwartz-Liebman.
1968.

Bottom left: Cotton chintz.
Everfast.
1964.

Top right: Cotton and nylon stretch denim.
Cone Mills.
1966.

Center right: Polyester blend.
Interchem.
1966.

Bottom right: Polyester blend.
Interchem.
1966.

Top left: Cotton chintz. Everfast. 1964.

Top right: Cotton chintz. Everfast. 1964.

Bottom left: Cotton chintz. Everfast. 1964.

Bottom right: Cotton chintz. Everfast. 1964.

157

Top left: 100% cotton.
Everfast.
1962.

Center left: Crepeset nylon styled by Prentiss-Lane, Inc.
Burlington for American Enka Corp.
1964.

Bottom left: 100% silk, created by Gourdon.
Kanebo.
1960.

Top right: Cotton chintz.
Everfast.
1964.

Center right: Cotton chintz.
Everfast.
1964.

Bottom right: "Airnyl" nylon taffeta.
Travis.
1965.

158

100% silk.
Late 1960s.

Wisteria.
Combé satin.
Everfast.
1966.

CHAPTER 9

PAISLEY

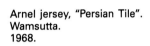

Arnel jersey, "Persian Tile".
Wamsutta.
1968.

100% cotton.
Early 1960s.

Opposite:
100% cotton.
Early 1960s

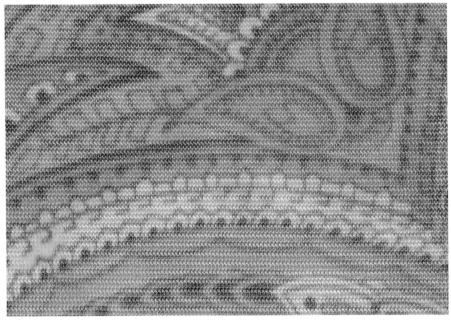

Arnel jersey, "Pastel Paisley".
Wamsutta.
1968.

Top left: 100% Acrilan printed knit. Triton. 1965.

Top right: Wool sheer open weave. Early 1960s.

Bottom left: Wool sheer open weave. Early 1960s.

Bottom right: Cotton blend chintz. 1960.

Cotton blend.
1960.

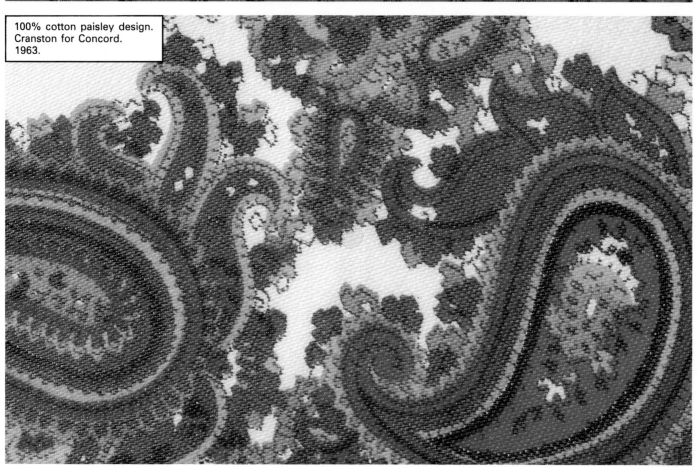

100% cotton paisley design.
Cranston for Concord.
1963.

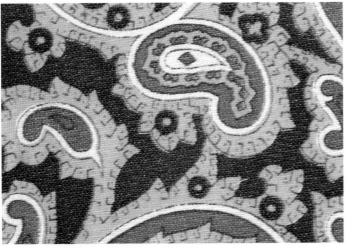

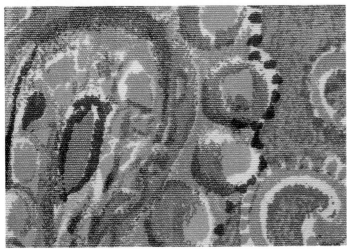

Top left: Blend and bonded.
Cranston Print Works.
1968.

Bottom left: 100% Supima cotton batiste, "Maharani's Robe".
Cranston.
1961.

Top right: 100% combed cotton, sateen print.
Lowenstein.
Mid 1960s.

Bottom right: Cotton.
Everfast.
1964.

Cotton.
Everfast.
1964.

100% cotton print.
Schumacher.
1961.

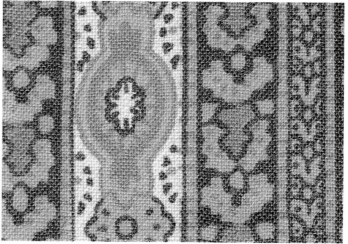

Printed foam laminate.
Riegel Textiles.
1962.

100% cotton print, "Prado
Tile".
Kenmill Textile Corporation.
1963.

100% silk Shantung.
Belding Corticelli.
1960.

Cotton.
Interchem.
1966.

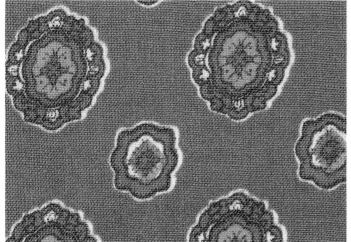

Cotton blend.
Mid 1960s.

Acetate and nylon blend.
Avisco.
1960.

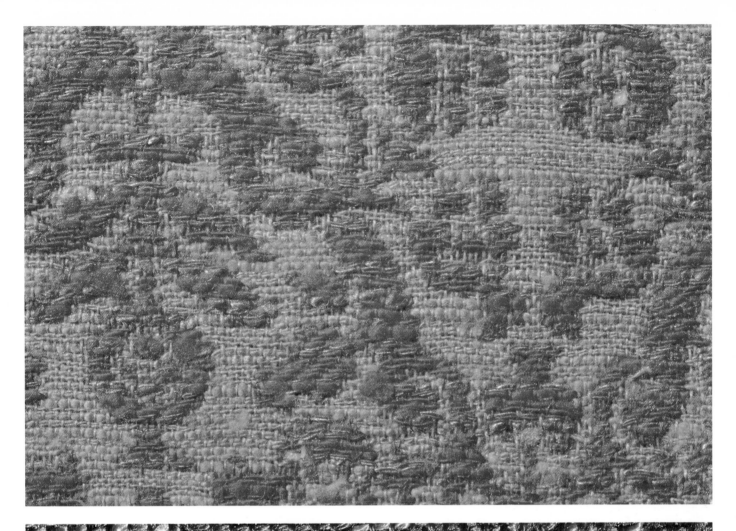

CHAPTER 10

PICTORIAL

Top left: 100% wool challis, by Leslie Tillett. Belle Fabrics. 1961.

Top right: 100% cotton, print. Fuller Fabrics. 1961.

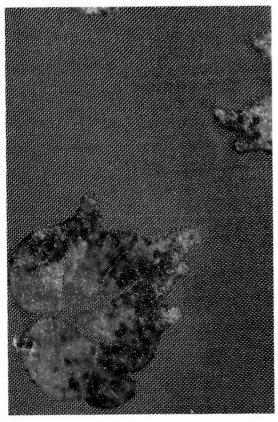

Bottom left: 100% nylon. Earl-Glo. 1965.

Bottom right: 67% stretch nylon, 33% stretch Dacron. Wamsutta. 1963.

Opposite page:
Top: 100% stretch nylon knit. Leumas Knitting Mills. 1969.

Bottom: 100% yarn-dyed stretch nylon. Leumas Mills. 1968.

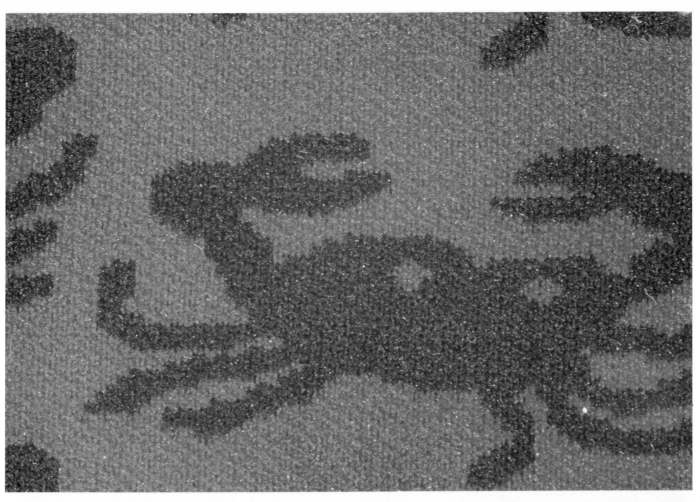

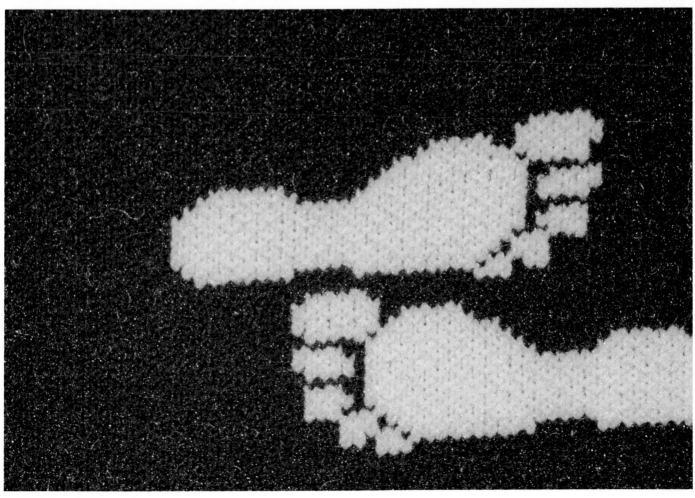

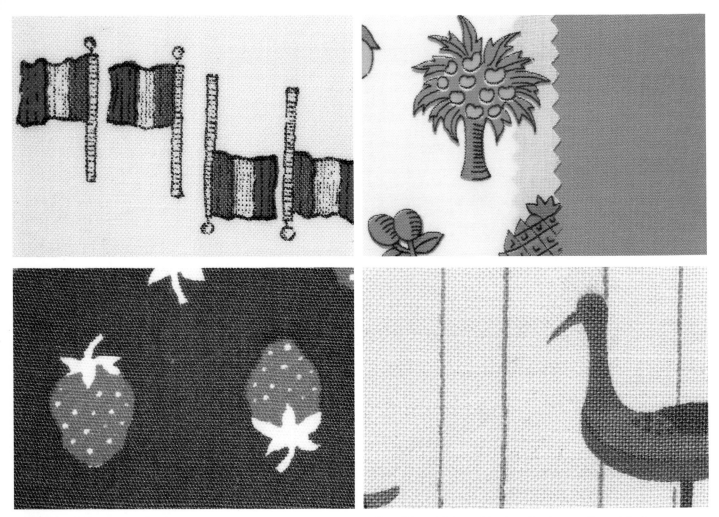

Top left: 100% cotton print.
Kenmill Textile Corporation.
1963.

Bottom left: 50/50 blend of Avril rayon and cotton.
M. Lowenstein & Sons.
1964.

Top right: 50/50 combination, Creslan acrylic and Avril.
Pacific Mills Division of M. Lowenstein.
1964.

Bottom right: Cotton.
Printed by Cranston.
Schwartz-Liebman.
1964.

172

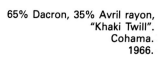

Caprolan printed crepe.
Maxwell Textiles.
1964.

65% Dacron, 35% Avril rayon,
"Khaki Twill".
Cohama.
1966.

55% Kodel, 45% Topel rayon.
Fabric by Travis.
J.P. Stevens Mill.
1960.

Rayon crepe.
Late 1960s.

173

Top: Cotton.
Aubrey Beardsley, Art Nouveau revival print.
Late 1960s.

Bottom left: Cotton.
Aubrey Beardsley, Art Nouveau revival print.
Late 1960s.

Center: Cotton.
Aubrey Beardsley, Art Nouveau revival print.
Late 1960s.

Bottom right: Cotton.
Aubrey Beardsley, Art Nouveau revival print.
Late 1960s.

BIBLIOGRAPHY

American Fabrics. New York: Doric Publishing Co., Issues 1960-1969.

Brown, Patty and Janett Rice. *Ready-to-Wear Apparel Analysis*. Upper Saddle River, New Jersey: Prentice-Hall, Inc., 1998.

Christie, Archibald H. *Pattern Design An Introduction To The Study of Formal Ornament*. New York: Dover Publications, Inc., 1969.

Demir, Ali and Hassan Mohamed Behery. *Synthetic Filament Yarn Texturing Technology*. Upper Saddle River, New Jersey: Prentice-Hall Inc., 1997.

Edelstein, Andrew J. *The Pop Sixties*. New York: World Almanac Publications, 1985.

Encyclopedia of Textiles, American Fabrics. Englewood Cliffs, New Jersey: Prentice-Hall, 1980.

Gioello, Debbie Ann. *Profiling Fabrics: Properties, Performance & Construction Techniques*. New York: Fairchild Publications, 1981.

Humphries, Mary. *Fabric Glossary*. Upper Saddle River, New Jersey: Prentice Hall, 1996.

Jackman, Dianne R. and Mary K. Dixon. *The Guide to Textiles for Interior Designers*. Winnipeg, Canada: Peguis Publishing Ltd., 1990.

Larsen, Jack Lenor. *The Dyer's Art: Ikat, Batik, Plangi.* New York: Van Nostrand Reinhold Co., 1976.

Lauterburg, Lotti. *Fabric Printing*. New York: Reinhold Publishing Corp., 1959.

Lobenthal, Joel. *Radical Rags Fashions of The Sixties*. New York: Abbeville Press, Inc. 1990.

Moncrieff, R.W. *Man-made Fibres*. New York: John Wiley & Sons Inc., 1987.

Placek, Karl J. *Ornaments and Designs*. New York: Bonanza Books, 1971.

Proud, Nora. *Introducing Textile Printing*. New York: Watson-Guptill Publications, 1968.

Reichman, Charles. *Knitting Dictionary*. New York: National Knitted Outerwear Association, 1966.

Robinson, Stuart. *A History of Dyed Textiles* . Cambridge, Massachusetts: The MIT Press, 1969.

Russ, Stephen. *Fabric Printing by Hand*. New York: Watson-Guptill Publications, 1965.

Tortora, Phyllis B. *Fairchild's Dictionary of Textiles*. Upper Saddle River, New Jersey: Prentice-Hall Inc., 1996.

-----. *Understanding Textiles*. Upper Saddle River, New Jersey: Prentice-Hall Inc., 1996.

Wilson, Kax. *A History of Textiles.* Boulder, Colorado: West View Press, Inc., 1979.

INDEX